Born in London, 4th August 1839. Educated at King's School, Canterbury, and Queen's College, Oxford, he became a Fellow of Brasenose and spent most of his life there, in the vacations travelling on the Continent or, latterly, living in London. As an undergraduate he became interested in art, literature and philosophy. He began his literary career in 1866 by contributing an essay on Coleridge to the *Westminster Review*, but it was the collection *Studies in the History of the Renaissance*, 1873, which first made his name. His other major works include the novel, *Marius the Epicurean*, 1885, and *Plato and Platonism*, 1893. He was made an honorary LL.D. of Glasgow in 1894 and died at Oxford on 30th July in the same year.

Walter Pater
Essays on Literature and Art

Edited by Jennifer Uglow

Dent, London
Rowman and Littlefield, Totowa, N. J.

© Introduction and notes, J. M. Dent & Sons Ltd, 1973
All rights reserved
Made in Great Britain
at the
Aldine Press · Letchworth · Herts
for
J. M. DENT & SONS LTD
Aldine House · Albemarle Street · London
This edition was first published in 1973
First published in the United States 1973
by ROWMAN AND LITTLEFIELD, Totowa, New Jersey

Dent edition
Hardback ISBN 0 460 10192 7

Rowman and Littlefield edition
Hardback ISBN 0/87471/395/1

Contents

Introduction

Outwardly the life of Walter Horatio Pater (1839–1894) was unevent-
ful, for the most important events of his life were internal intellectual
and aesthetic experiences. Time and again his contemporaries
describe him in terms of a mask; Henry James, writing to Edmund
Gosse in 1894 about the latter's study of Pater in *Critical Kit Kats*
concludes:

> how curiously negative and faintly grey he, after all telling, remains! I
> think he has had—will have had—the most exquisite literary fortune: i.e.
> to have taken it out all, wholly, exclusively, with the pen (the style, the
> genius) and absolutely not at all with the person. He is the mask without the
> face, and there isn't in his total superficies a tiny point of vantage for the
> newspaper to flap its wings on. (*The Letters of Henry James*. Ed. Lubbock, 1920)

The personal reticence for which he was renowned acted as a shell to
protect his sensibility and many of his inhibitions and obsessions were
to find some release in his art.

From childhood he knew what it was like to feel alone; his father
died when he was three, his mother while he was at school, and
although he was to live with his sisters for much of his adult life they
were often abroad during his childhood and adolescence. He had
therefore early experience of the sense of loss and transience which
was to figure so largely in his work. Some impression of his early
development may be gained from the semi-autobiographical portrait
'The Child in the House'.[1]

Two more imaginary portraits, 'Emerald Uthwart' and 'An
English Poet',[2] give us an idea of his life at school, at King's College,
Canterbury. He was not strong and was too reserved to enjoy the
rougher elements of public school life, but he found pleasure in
reading and in the beauty of the nearby cathedral. While at school
he met Keble, then in retirement at Hursley, a meeting which
contributed to his current ambitions, to be a priest and to be a
poet. He wrote a considerable amount of poetry between the ages of
16 and 21; but in 1860 he burnt his manuscript book of poems in

disapproval of their Christian tone, with all his other religious books.[3]

For in 1858 Pater had gone to Queen's College, Oxford to read Greats, and soon, to the horror of his friends, he swung from piety to scepticism although for a time he persisted in his ambition to become ordained. In his finals he obtained second class honours but in 1862 he acquired a fellowship at Brasenose due, it was said, to his knowledge of German and French philosophy. He remained there until 1881 when he resigned his tutorship in order to devote himself to the writing of *Marius the Epicurean* (1885). His later years were occupied in writing and his time was divided between Oxford and London.

Pater's personality baffled those who knew him; he was shy and retiring, self-conscious about his appearance, often crossing the road to avoid greeting acquaintances. Many saw him as the weary, murmuring high priest of the aesthetic movement, and he is caricatured as such in the person of Mr Rose in W. H. Mallock's *New Republic* (1877). Max Beerbohm was one person whose early aesthetic aspirations were dashed when he found Pater's lectures completely inaudible. 'Giving lectures for him,' Max remarked, 'was a form of self-communion. He whispered them.' Yet there are also many stories of his kindness, loyalty, and—surprising to those who know him only through his writing—his keen wit and buoyant sense of humour. The ambivalent impression he created in life is reflected in the complexity of his work.

The youthful ideal of culture

Pater lacked the scholarship and also the heartiness of the traditional Oxford don. The 'revolutionary' views of his early essays shocked academic stalwarts such as Benjamin Jowett, Master of Balliol, and he soon acquired a certain notoriety in the university. Yet he does belong to a specific Oxford tradition. The aesthetic movement, like the theological Oxford Movement, looked to the past as a guide to the future, rejecting the prized John Bull insularity and stressing instead the links with the European and, in effect, Catholic, past. Pater shares with Newman and Arnold a respect for this wider heritage as well as a faith in the spiritual values of a liberal education, a belief in the value of 'urbanity'—a sensitive sultured temperament —and a certain academic elitism. Their ideal was typified by Arnold's vision of Oxford itself:

... steeped in sentiment as she lies, spreading her gardens to the moonlight, and whispering from her towers the last enchantments of the Middle Age, who will deny that Oxford, by her ineffable charm, keeps ever calling us nearer to the true goal of all of us, to the ideal, to perfection. (*Essays in Criticism*, 1865).

Pater's aesthetic was firmly in line with late Romantic theory. This was recognized by one of the most perceptive of his contemporary critics, John Morley, who traced a line from the Oxford Movement, through Ruskin, the Pre-Raphaelites and Morris, to *The Renaissance*, concluding:

This more recent pagan movement ... is equally a protest against the mechanical and graceless formalism of the modern era ... equally a craving for the infusion of something more harmonius and beautiful about the bare lines of daily living. (*Fortnightly Review*, No. XIII, 1873).

Yet the antecedents of Pater's theory can be traced back still further to the Romantics themselves. Pater had a lasting respect for the Romantic assertion of the importance of intuition and imagination as opposed to the rational philosophy and codified standards of taste of the eighteenth century, and he can thus respond warmly to Coleridge in so far as the latter's work reflects 'the power of a sincere effort towards the ideal life, of even a temporary escape of the spirit from routine'. For Pater the peculiar power of nineteenth-century poetry lay in the combination of vision with observation, which gave it a new interpretative force. The English tradition mingles in his philosophy of art with elements more usually identified with the French Romantics, such as the appreciation of the bizarre or macabre in art and the emphasis on stylistic precision.[4] These strands combine with the influence of the German Hellenists' ideal of total harmony and thought and with his personal interpretation of current philosophical theories, to produce a comprehensive and, with a few exceptions, a consistent aesthetic.

Pater felt that the appreciation of art must be fresh, personal and direct; this meant that the reader, observer, or listener had to discard not only all preconceptions about standards of taste, but all philosophical preconceptions as well. This much is clear from the early essay on Coleridge (p. 1), where all idealism seemed to him to limit arbitrarily the scope and richness of man's experience. At the beginning of his career Pater was to follow Arnold's suggestion that the only formula which could truly have a claim on the spiritual life of modern man was that of perfection through culture, the study of the best that had been thought and said in the world. For Arnold had asserted that culture was seeking the answer to the question of the attainment of perfection:

through all the voices of human experience which have been heard upon it, of art, science, philosophy, history, as well as religion, in order to give a greater fulness and certainty to its solution. (*Culture and Anarchy*, 1869).

'Coleridge' also marks Pater's conscious embrace of the relative spirit. In these early essays he was profoundly influenced by the discoveries of nineteenth-century science which, he felt, had proved that all life, even the inner mental processes, was in a state of flux in which personal identity was in danger of disintegrating. In this condition all fixed views, including dogma, must be untenable and the faculty for discovering truth is 'recognized as a power of distinguishing and fixing delicate and fugitive detail'.

The theme of individual identity, truthful perception in an ever-changing world, is pursued further in 'The Conclusion' (p.39). Here Pater says that awareness of the inner self can be discovered, and life enriched, through intense perception. His theory is similar to that advanced by contemporary Oxford Hegelians, and indeed several leaders of this school, Edward Caird, T. H. Green, Bernard Bosanquet and William Wallace were among Pater's personal friends.[5] From his superficial knowledge of Hegel's philosophy Pater adopted the theory that knowledge, 'the conscious certainty of self', was the opposite to 'fear', insecurity in the face of the flux of life. Pater's search for unity and identity through 'impassioned contemplation' echoes Hegel's search for the unity of 'Geist', the principle of constant evolution under the guise of random change. Pater interprets the theory of perception thus; through intense concentration on a fleeting impression one makes contact with external reality, then, in analysing the impression the mind becomes aware of its own response and thereby of its own nature. Ultimately, through comparison of such responses in memory, one can define an ordered pattern beneath seeming chaos. The passion for art has the greatest potential for staving off the sense of transience because in art the perceptions of a highly sensitive mind are already ordered; we are confronted with a reality already refined and we are also able to reach the personality behind the work.

The 'Conclusion' was withdrawn from the second edition of *The Renaissance* because of criticism that its advocacy of living for the moment might mislead youth.[6] Pater himself later realized the narrowness of his early position and, as he points out in a note to the modified form of the piece in the third edition, he explains his position more fully in *Marius the Epicurean*. In the novel he is anxious to stress that it is not pleasure but insight he seeks through culture and he acknowledges the limitations of his early statements. The phrase 'Art for Art's sake' is often tossed out in connection with Pater but it should be made clear that it cannot be used without careful modification. When Swinburne introduced Gautier's phrase into English criticism in his *William Blake* (1868) he used it to proclaim the complete supremacy of form over subject-matter—'Save the shape and art will take care of the soul for you'—and to stress the total separation of art from any moral or didactic purpose. Pater, too, lauds perfection of form, but for him the value of art is not its separation from life, but its very power to enrich 'the moments as they pass'. It would be quite inconceivable for Pater to utter the credo of Swinburne's hero in *The Chronicle of Tebaldeo Tebaldei*, 'a beautiful line drawn is more than a life saved; a pleasant perfume smelt is better than a soul redeemed'. Even in reading the early work it is important to realize that for both Arnold and Pater perfection through culture, despite its 'ivory tower' implications, did not in theory cut off the observer or critic from the world of sense and human action.

In 'Winckelmann' (p. 27) Pater elaborates on the power of art to offer an escape from temporality and from the inexorability of natural law. He also stresses here the part which the senses, free from shame and superimposed moral attitudes, must play in the appreciation of art. Both Pater and Arnold felt that 'Hellenism'—disinterested intellectual curiosity and clarity, the desire for beauty—could redress an imbalance in contemporary attitudes of mind, too dominated by 'Hebraic' values, where all other sides of one's being were sacrificed to the religious side, and where systems of conduct and moral codes threatened to become more important than the spirit which originally inspired them. Pater employs the argument although he does not use the specific term 'Hebraic'.

The seminal idea was Arnold's but, despite variations of emphasis, he never denigrated the Hebraic side of the opposition, as Pater seemed to do in his early work. Furthermore, Arnold had a declared social aim as well as a personal motive in championing culture. He felt that 'perfection is not possible while the individual is isolated' for in his view culture embraced all desire to clear away misery and leave the world a better place, so that he could assert in *Culture and Anarchy* that 'culture moves by the force, not merely or primarily of the scientific passion for knowledge but also of the moral and social passion for doing good'. Pater, in these opening essays, locates the value of an education through culture solely in the benefit to the individual soul. This is yet another reason for the later modification of his views.

The aim of such an education was the achievement of a certain kind of temperament; sensitive, detached, flexible in thought and feeling. As both Arnold and Pater identify this temperament with the mood of Hellenism it is worth exploring further what they mean by this term. In contrast to Christian, particularly Puritan, exclusiveness and provinciality Arnold had turned to 'the finely tempered nature' which he felt to be the product of classical Greek culture and to the best art and poetry of the Greeks, in which religion and poetry are one, in which the idea of beauty and of a human nature perfect on all sides adds to itself a religious and devout energy and works in the strength of that. (*Culture and Anarchy*)

In 'Coleridge' Pater had maintained that the value of religion lay in the states of mind which worship induced rather than in any doctrinal element. He claimed that these mental states could be maintained without the dogma which hitherto accompanied them; they could be gained especially from the study of great human achievement in any sphere, and from the supreme achievement of Greek culture in particular. But Arnold had held, as had Newman, a view of Greek art and religion as embodiments of carefree serenity which Pater could not accept. His Hellenism is more complex than Arnold's, for he recognizes in Greek myth and art romantic elements which fused with formal simplicity and restraint to produce an era of cultural harmony. For Pater the lasting value of Hellenic culture and religion is that they are informed by profound ideals which are not imposed separately by the intellect, but which arise gradually and directly from concrete experience, from a sensory and spiritual appreciation of nature and humanity.

Pater's view of art and literature as giving continuity to human experience through time is related to his view of history. His historical approach is coloured by his understanding of the theory of evolution and he adopts the idea of development by antagonism where each epoch may be considered as holding in varying proportions opposing and permanent aspects of human nature or of abstract principles. Later in his career, in *Plato and Platonism* (1893), Pater calls modern theories of development 'old Heracliteanism awake once more in a new world and grown to full proportions', and curiously allies Darwin and Hegel as joint exponents of the theory of gradual progression through constant change.[7] The fusion of influences is complicated still further in 'Coleridge' and the other early essays by echoes of Comte.[8] A developmental approach to history is not novel in nineteenth-century criticism, and is found, among other places, in J. S. Mill's idea of critical and organic periods and in Newman's *Development of Christian Doctrine* (1845). Arnold also employs the idea in 'The Function of Criticism' (1865) and in the comparison between ages of sense and ages of the heart in 'Pagan and Medieval Religious Sentiment' (1865).

The dialectical approach allows both Pater and Arnold to find the mood of their own age, 'the modern spirit' in sporadic outbursts before the nineteenth century; in fifth-century Athens, in the Rome of the Antonines, and in the Renaissance. Thus in 'Winckelmann', where Pater adopts temporarily Hegel's idea of the sequential development of the arts, each age is seen to contain the seeds of a different cultural flowering. The most interesting periods in cultural history must be those in which a stage in the development of the world spirit coincides with a high degree of artistic enterprise and expertise as in the Renaissance, and such ages, because of their cultural harmony, will also produce 'wondrous personalities'.

The dialectic of art

The 'School of Giorgione' (p. 43), included in the 1877 edition of *The Renaissance*, opens with a plea for the recognition by critics of the essential quality of each artistic medium—for example in painting the elusive 'pictorial' quality which is neither technical merit nor simple illustrative accuracy. Pater felt that each art form could translate imaginative thought in different ways, addressing not the senses or the intellect alone but the 'imaginative reason through the senses'. Great art will hold in balance opposing elements of matter and form, reality and subjective vision. Thus the task of the artist is to express his dream or idea in limited line and colour, while that of the sculptor is to achieve a fusion between the 'palpable and limited human form and the floating essence it is to contain'. This theory of containment and fusion lies behind Pater's advocacy of lyric poetry with its condensed suggestiveness, his sensitivity to the demands of the different media and his famous statement 'all art constantly aspires to the condition of music'. For music is the art form in which form and content are seemingly indivisible and it is also, by its very nature, the emblem of harmony.

'Giorgione', in the detailed analysis of the Venetian school which follows the extract included in this volume, also contains the highest claim Pater was to make for the significance of art and literature in the interpretation of the moment. The power of dramatic poetry lies in the fact that it

presents us with a kind of profoundly significant and animated instants, a mere gesture, a look, a smile perhaps—some brief and wholly concrete moment—into which, however, all the interests and effects of a long history have condensed themselves, and which seem to absorb past and present in an intense consciousness of the present. (*The Renaissance*, 2nd edition, 1878)

Here is a direct statement of Pater's ideal of the blended impression, a harmony which transcends time. Art solves the problem of combining the movement of the flux of life with the desire to arrest the moments as they pass, for each instant is held yet animated, implying the flow of life before and after it.

Just as Pater traced antagonism in history so he envisaged opposing forces in art and the creative process. This opposition, he believed, sprang from a basic duality in human nature—a constant struggle between the principles of motion and rest, which could only be resolved in a perfectly balanced personality. This scheme provides a key to Pater's critical position in many essays. Occasionally he describes the two sides in detail under different names; romantic and classic in the 'Postscript' (p. 48), Ionian and Doric, Asiatic and European in 'The Marbles of Ægina' (p. 59). Elsewhere he applies his theory of opposition and synthesis to the work of individuals, 'curiosity and the desire for beauty' in Leonardo, 'strength and sweetness' in Michaelangelo, the grave and gay elements in Lamb's essays, the Italian grace and French design in du Bellay's verse.

This insistence on balance lies at the root of Pater's preoccupation with style in the works he explores. Style, as he explains it in the essay of that name (p. 61), involves at its best an exact correspondence between the vision and the medium chosen to express it, so that a good literary style is that which most truthfully reveals the writer's 'sense of fact'. It is therefore transparent in that the words are identical with the thought and have no superfluous colouring. This truth to inner vision, he concludes, means that 'the style is the man'. Despite his admiration for Flaubert he cannot accept the French novelist's assertion of the impersonality of art, although, because he does not wish to differ from his hero, he ends up typically trying to resolve their two views, claiming paradoxically that style is 'impersonal' simply because it is true to the individual view.

It transpires that Pater, with his constant awareness of the struggle involved in artistic creation, has a far more strenuous view of art than the languid aestheticism usually accredited to him. In 'Style' he insists that 'Soul', the element of inspiration, must always be controlled and ordered by 'Mind', the element of reason and structural ability. In 'Coleridge', at the start of his career, Pater had rejected the idea of the artist as a mere 'mechanical agent' of inspiration.

Culture, at least, values even in transcendent works of art the power of the understanding in them, their logical process of construction, the spectacle of supreme intellectual dexterity which they afford. (p. 17)

This view is repeated in 'Style' written twenty-two years later, and was indeed a constant tenet of his criticism.

One more point, of a rather different order, must be made about the critical approach revealed in this essay. It seems to contain in its final stages a distinction which completely overturns Pater's claim to relative criticism—the judgment of a work in relation to circumstance, personality, artistic medium and tradition—and of his claim to value a work in terms of formal truth to vision without absolute standards. Having landed perfection of form he suddenly declares that ultimately it is by the subject and not by the presentation that we should judge great art:

It is on the quality of the matter it informs or controls, its compass, its variety, its alliance to great ends, or the depth of the note of revolt, or the largeness of hope in it, that the greatness of literary art depends. (p. 78).

Initially this seems out of character but in fact such a distinction is employed in most of his criticism. He uses a double classification which in its simplest form can be put thus: good art is to be found wherever form embodies an individual view, so an artist like Botticelli or Lamb is to be valued because of the unique nature of his contribution. Great art is to be found where supreme stylistic control is allied to a vision which reveals a fundamental concern with permanent human problems and aspirations. This is the work of the great masters such as Wordsworth, Goethe, Leonardo and Shakespeare. But the very definite statement of this position in 'Style' and the examples Pater chooses, *Paradise Lost*, *The Divine Comedy*, *Les Misérables*, above all *The English Bible*, show how far he had moved since his early declaration that art is to be enjoyed 'simply for those moments' sake'.

Critical method

Pater's critical method, like his aesthetic theory, is conditioned by his rejection of traditional standards and attitudes. His approach to his task is even more personal than Arnold's, for at least at the start of his career Pater recognized no absolutes, while Arnold never abandoned his belief in the value of accepted critical standards, as is evident from 'The Literary Influence of Academies'. Pater tells us in the 'Preface' (p. 79) that 'beauty, like all other qualities presented to human experience, is relative; and the definition of it becomes unmeaning and useless in proportion to its abstractness'. The critic should not begin with an assumption that one school, period or style is superior to another, but should look for excellence in every age. Starting from assessment of a work in relation to the circumstances in which it was produced, he will come to the realization that true genius is 'above the age', its quality is timeless and universal. In one of his last works *Plato and Platonism* (see p. 82) he still clings to the idea that to understand and fully appreciate a work one must recreate the age and even the personality of its creator.

Denied the support of established standards of taste, what criterion is the critic to use as a guide? Again Pater is definite; he adopts Arnold's stated aim, 'to see the object as it really is', but he insists that a precondition of this is to know one's own impression as it really is. But when Pater says that the first question to be asked must be 'What effect does it really produce on *me*?', he is not, like Wilde after him, saying that the subjective response of the critic is more important than the work itself, but simply stressing that the essentials of criticism are honesty, self-awareness and a lack of preconceived judgments. He writes in the belief that the function of a critic is to share his discoveries with others for their interest and enlightenment. He seeks to fulfil Arnold's ideal of one who imparts knowledge 'as a sort of companion and clue, not as an abstract law-giver'.

As a guide to method Pater turns to the only process of analysis which seems to him unassailable, the technique of scientific observation. In attempting to transfer these techniques to criticism he even adopts their terminology. Thus the critics' aim is to find the 'formula', the 'active principle', in the work of artist or writer, and 'his end is reached when he has disengaged that virtue and noted it, as a chemist notes some natural element for himself and for others'. The critic's chief tool in this analysis is not a correct intellectual definition of beauty but a 'certain kind of temperament, the power of being deeply moved by the presence of beautiful objects'.

The dangers implicit in such an approach are obvious, for the ability to experience intensely is seldom matched, even in the most self-aware of men, by the ability to analyse dispassionately. Indeed the critic may not be aware of, or at least unwilling to recognize, the reason for this attraction to certain artists, styles and subjects. The desire to recreate the impression may lead him, moreover, to the use of over-colourful language, while the effort to isolate the essential 'charm' of a work can result in over-emphasis on the emotional as opposed to the intellectual content of a work. Furthermore, the desire to trace a work to the sources of creation within the personality may involve a manipulation of biography. This is true of Pater's own work; he ignores elements of an artist's life which seem to jar with his initial impression and tends to treat his subjects as though they were fictional characters. But Pater's sensitivity and caution help him to avoid most of these pitfalls except on isolated occasions.

Literary criticism

One corollary of impressionistic criticism is the lack of emphasis on technical and academic data. Pater certainly did not despise the more pedestrian aspects of scholarship and made careful notes of literary and artistic conventions, but he insisted that antiquarian interest alone could not make a work a fit subject for aesthetic criticism. For this it must possess a 'real, direct, aesthetic charm'. The first essay in this section is a study of the French six-teenth-century poet Joachim du Bellay (p. 83), a writer whose work possessed for Pater both historic interest and considerable literary merit.

Part of du Bellay's attraction for Pater lay in the fact that he could see in his work signs of the transition from one era to another; the end of Italian dominance and the birth of a new national school of poetry in France. Pater associates the poets of the Pléiade with the end of the Renaissance, finding in their poetry symbols of age and decadence, but he also views them in relation to the future, tracing a link with nineteenth-century poetry in the 'intimité', the quality of subjective personal experience in du Bellay's lyrics. He even analyses the poet's malaise in terms very close to those he had applied to Coleridge. He is also concerned with the national importance of the Pléiade, moving from initial discussion of the fusion of Italian and French influences in the artistic achievement of the period to a concentration on the efforts of Ronsard and his colleagues to establish the vernacular as a fit medium for poetry and to 'adjust the existing French culture to the rediscovered classical culture'.

The essay is as much a study of cultural history, tied to a portrait of a personality, as an analytical survey of a particular poet. But when Pater does turn to the poetry he immediately identifies the strength of du Bellay's work, the taut structure and suggestiveness of a lyric which may at first sight seem trivial. The few examples are well chosen and 'Le Vanneur' in particular illustrates both the strength of the lyric and the grounds of its appeal to Pater—its ability to capture the unique moment of experience without descending to frozen formality.

In his study of William Morris (p. 95), Pater is also examining a link between the nineteenth century and the past, from the other end of the time spectrum. Although he concentrates on individual works he considers Morris important as representative of a literary coterie whose work embodies a particular variety of nineteenth-century imaginative expression. In the first edition of *Appreciations* he con-densed his earlier review of Morris's poems to emphasize their representative quality, calling the new version 'Aesthetic Poetry'. One of the weaknesses of the essay is that it has two slightly different subjects, not very clearly defined: Morris's reaction to the medieval and classical past as it finds expression in his verse and Pater's own ideas of the sharply differing cultures of the two periods. But above all this essay, and the companion study of Rossetti, reveal Pater's fascination with the sensuous, atmospheric quality of poetry. He sets out to evoke the mood of the poems he analyses and he does suggest effectively the dreamlike impression created by the precise convoluted detail in the work of Pre-Raphaelite writers and artists, and the artifice with which they create an ideal world out of myth and legend. The language employed is more highly coloured than anything in Pater's later work, apart from isolated examples in *The Renaissance*. It appears that he regretted his extravagance, for the essay was withdrawn from later editions of *Appreciations*, possibly because of the anti-Christian bias detected in his provocative analysis of the relation between medieval religion and courtly love, and in such phrases as 'monasticism is simply a beautiful disease', a remark which understandably caused a certain stir.

The essay on Wordsworth which follows (p. 103) provides a strong contrast in subject and treatment. Again Pater relates the poet to his philosophical and literary context, but his stated aim here is to find the 'essence' of Wordsworth's genius. His opening remarks on the difference between the inspired and prosaic elements in Wordsworth's work are not just examples of the Victorian love of anthologizing, but a prelude to a precise definition of Wordsworth's achievement. The study moves towards an analysis of Wordsworth as a meditative poet, whose philosophy of a life spirit uniting the world of natural objects and the world of human society arises directly from intense contemplation of external reality. Pater describes with sympathy the poet's semi-mystical intuition of the forces at work in nature and man and for him Wordsworth stood, with Goethe, as a central type of the detached, disinterested genius. Pater sees in Wordsworth's 'impassioned contemplation' a supreme example of the intuition's ability to reach the perception of a principle of unity beyond that attainable by rational analysis alone.

Although the attitudes of the English Romantics permeate Pater's criticism, the studies of Coleridge and Wordsworth represent his only serious attempts to define the strengths and weaknesses of the movement. Elsewhere he comments on Shelley, Blake, Keats and Browning in passing, while his only lengthy discussion of Browning is in a rather superficial review of a critical study by Symons.

The study of *Measure for Measure* (p. 117) shows a similar preoccupation with the unity which a creative imagination can impose upon disparate elements. Pater's appraisal of the play is free from the moral indignation and bewilderment with which his predecessors and contemporaries had viewed it. He appreciates that the characters act in accordance with the interior movement of the play and that in the heightened world of drama, psychology is accurate not in realistic detail but in poetic representation of human drives, instincts and emotions. He is alert to the exigencies and advantages of the dramatic form; the suggestions which can be evoked by grouping of characters, variation of mood, pace and scene, and the possibility of creating a unique world of action which is yet a microcosm of the human condition. In his survey of the complex elements woven into the action of *Measure for Measure* Pater relates the play to its source and draws illuminating parallels with Webster and with the old moralities. Finally he is able to state clearly the qualities which, for him, give the play its permanent relevance—the portrayal of ethical truths not through dogmatic statement but through a pattern of human relationships and action.

Measure for Measure shows the strength of Pater's method while 'Charles Lamb' (p. 125) reveals its weakness. That Pater could produce sensitive and interesting criticism of prose writers is evident from his studies of essayists such as Coleridge, Browne and Montaigne. Here he makes a serious attempt to define the peculiar tone of Lamb's work, the combination of grave and gay, the dark undercurrents beneath the whimsical anecdotes, but his sympathy for his subject is such that interpretation gives way to sentimental evocation of Lamb's personality and tragic situation. Pater saw Lamb, like du Bellay, as representative of a transitional age, when the urbanity and rational religion of the eighteenth century was giving way to the more earnest philosophy and staider manners of the nineteenth, and as representative of a particular place; the fringes of London where 'quaint suburban pastorals' are given grandeur by the looming city in the background. But this time the description of the historical context seems more of an occasion for nostalgia than an aid to understanding the writer's work.

Furthermore it is clear that Pater felt a personal affinity with Lamb, both as a man and as a writer. His definitions of Lamb's achievement, 'tracking with an attention always alert, the whole process of their production to its starting point in the deep places of the mind' parallels his own stated critical aim, while the analysis of the latent self-portraiture in the work of all essay writers is an unconscious commentary on the effect produced by his own writing:

What he designs is to give you himself, to acquaint you with his likeness; but must do this, if at all, indirectly, being indeed always more or less reserved, for himself and his friends. (p. 131)

The reviews of the two late nineteenth-century writers included in this volume, Mary Ward and Oscar Wilde, reveal a more stringent

approach. Pater often lacked confidence when reviewing his contemporaries—his innate timidity and politeness seem to swamp his
judgment. The result can vary from non-committal reporting, as in
his reviews of the French writers Fabre and Filon, to a surplusage
of polite compliment as in 'Mr Gosse's Poems'.[9] But the two novels
reviewed here reflect contrasting elements of the Victorian literary
scene, the theological debate and the aesthetic movement, about
both of which Pater was deeply concerned. In his discussion of *Robert
Elsmere* (p. 135) his chief interest is in the predicament of the hero, one
common to many Victorian intellectuals and perhaps to Pater
himself. In his insistence that doubt is preferable to outright rejection,
as the former leaves room for hope, and in his assertion that such
hopeful sceptics must surely form the backbone of the Church, critics
have seen a reflection of his own move towards religious orthodoxy in
later life. It is interesting to compare this review with his attitude to
Montaigne in *Gaston de Latour*. His judgment helps to explain how
Pater, a confessed sceptic like Montaigne, could, like him, continue
throughout life to be devout in practice:

A lowly philosophy of ignorance would not be likely to disallow or discredit
whatever intimations there might be, in the experience of the wise or of the
simple, in favour of a venerable religion, which from its long history had
come to seem like a growth of nature . . . to deny, at all events would only
be 'to *limit* the mind by negation'. (*Gaston de Latour*, 1896)

The second review, that of *Dorian Gray* (p. 142) helps us to define
Pater's relationship to Wilde. Their names are often wrongly linked
as joint leaders of the aesthetic movement, and indeed the philosophy
of *The Renaissance* and, surprisingly, of *Marius the Epicurean* have been
blamed for contributing to the 'untidy lives' (as T. S. Eliot put it) of
the poets and writers of the 'Nineties. Wilde certainly acknowledged
a great debt to Pater; and Pater appreciated Wilde's critical insight
in *The Decay of Lying*, was entertained by his wit and paradox, and
admired his skill in creating character and atmosphere in the novel.
But in fact their attitudes to life and art are rather different as Pater
is quick to point out. In his view Wilde fails to show the true Epicureanism portrayed in *Marius*, for his heroes lose their sense of
sin and thus sink to lower levels of development rather than
rising to 'a complete and harmonious development of man's entire
organism'.

Pater's alertness to the moral element in *Dorian Gray* which had
been ignored by other contemporary critics, shows his deliberate
detachment from the assumptions and fashions of his age. In all his
criticism his sensitivity to historical and literary contexts, combined

with his concern for unprejudiced analysis of the work before him, does enable him to pinpoint what he sees as the essential quality of a work. But, as has been noted before, he is equally vulnerable to the weakness inherent in his critical approach. Paradoxically, his concentration on extracting the essence, the underlying unity in a writer's achievement, does not often lead to the analysis of details one would expect from the 'Preface', for that is a preliminary stage. Instead it usually results in a broad general exposition. The effect of such criticism is more impressionistic than 'scientific', and in attempting to recreate the dominant tone in a book or personality Pater can be led to extremes of expression, as in the extravagant metaphors of 'Aesthetic Poetry', or to extremes of identification, as in 'Charles Lamb'.

But while he may not always remain true to the precepts of his critical method his adherence to his principles of aesthetic theory is constant. Although his attitude towards religious faith becomes more flexible he holds to the idea of an education through culture even in his review of *Dorian Gray*. In 'Wordsworth' and 'Measure for Measure' in particular, he concentrates on the educative power of the great artist, and it is notable that he considers this to be a 'moral power', a description consistent with the views expressed in 'Style'. A study of art and literature can foster the detachment and sensitivity of temperament which allow the observer to judge the world without prejudice, and which therefore lead to right action. Thus in 'Wordsworth' Pater writes:

That the end of life is not action but contemplation—*being* as distinct from *doing*—a certain disposition of the mind: is, in some shape or other, the principle of all the higher morality.... To treat life in the spirit of art, is to make life a thing in which means and ends are identified: to encourage such treatment, the true moral significance of art and poetry. (p. 115)

and in *Measure for Measure* he sees the embodiment of his earlier plea in 'Coleridge' for a finer and more flexible moral judgment.

All the essays, in different ways, reveal Pater's preoccupation with balance and harmony. He himself was well aware of the tensions and forces which were combining to create what he called 'our curious, complex, aspiring age', and he knew that these tensions were reflected in his works and in his temperament. His aim, in criticism and later philosophical fiction, was to reconcile opposing elements: scientific 'fact' with the truth of art, intellectual honesty with human compassion and imaginative vision, the Hellenic ideal of form with Romantic 'soul'. While his vaunted objectivity is occasionally threatened by temperamental inclinations and by the desire to 'appreciate' rather than judge a work, in the end he makes few false estimates. His freedom from prejudice is seen in his unfashionable championship of artists and writers such as Botticelli and Browne, while his lack of provinciality is evident in his sensitive appraisal in passing of figures from very different cultures: Apuleius, Montaigne, Bruno, Heine, Stendhal, Verlaine and many others.

Pater's criticism, which seeks the blended impression, harmony rather than definition, does not provide us with authoritative judgments, but with suggestive, personal interpretation. It is his relative approach, his awareness of a work in relation to personality and to social and historical context, his deep concern for humanistic and cultural values, and above all, the integrity of his approach which explain the influences he exerted at the time and on the critics who succeeded him.

1 *Miscellaneous Studies*, 1895.

2 Ibid., and *Fortnightly Review*, 1931.

3 Thomas Wright in *The Life of Walter Pater* (1907) suggests this was done in emulation of a similar act in Goethe's *Wahrheit und Dichtung*, which Pater had recently read. Only one complete poem of Pater's survives: *The Chant of the Celestial Sailors*, a slight piece in which robust rhythms, stock imagery and diction, combine with sentimental religiosity. In places the imagery is reminiscent of Keble's *Hymns for Emigrants*. The following verses are typical:

> Every wave behind us glancing
> Wears a crest of snow white foam,
> Like the matin clouds advancing
> In the blue ethereal dome.
>
> In the stillness tall and stately
> Soars our mast in solitude,
> Steadfast as the mountain pine-tree
> Solemn like the Holy Rood.
> Homeward, to the shore Celestial! Onward
>   to the silver strand!
> Homeward! Homeward! Gentle brothers,
>   to the tranquil morning land.

4 e.g. Baudelaire, *Exposition Universelle*, 1855 ('Le Beau est toujours bizarre'), and Gautier, *Emaux et Camées*, 1852.

5 For an interesting analysis of Pater's debt to Hegel see Anthony Ward, *Walter Pater, The Idea in Nature*, 1966.

6 An example of this criticism is contained in a letter to Pater from John Wordsworth, a former pupil, later Bishop of Salisbury. Speaking of the apparent denial of religious and moral principles in the *Conclusion* he writes: 'Could you have known the dangers into which you were likely to lead minds weaker than your own you would, I believe, have paused'. *Letters of Walter Pater*, ed. Evans, 1970.

7 '. . . it is the burden of Hegel on the one hand, to whom nature, and art, and polity, and philosophy, aye, and religion too, each in its long historic series, are but so many moves in the secular process of the eternal mind; and on the other hand of Darwin and Darwinism, for which the "type" itself properly *is* not but is only always *becoming*.' *Plato and Platonism*, 1893.

Pater also refers to Heraclitus' saying, 'everything vanishes and nothing remains', at the beginning of the 'Conclusion', and discusses his philosophy of stability behind the flux of life in *Marius the Epicurean*, Vol. I, Ch. VIII.

8 Comte saw the development of the human spirit as a three stage process: the Theological stage where control is believed to lie with supernatural powers; the Metaphysical, where abstract laws such as 'Nature' are substituted for divine laws; and the Positive, where facts are studied in relation to each other so that society can be studied as analytically as science. He further distinguished between 'organic' states of society, where power and ability are united in the ruling class, and 'critical' states, where this unified control is upset. Both he and Mill considered the nineteenth century to be a 'critical' stage, because traditional modes of control (the Church, the autocratic state) had been challenged but not replaced.

9 For several such reviews see *Essays from the Guardian*, 1901.

Select Bibliography

WORKS

The Renaissance. 1873; second edition 1877 ('Conclusion' omitted);
third edition 1888.
Marius the Epicurean. 1885.
Imaginary Portraits. 1887.
Appreciations. 1889; second edition 1890 ('Aesthetic Poetry' omitted).
Plato and Platonism. 1893.
Greek Studies. Ed. C. L. Shadwell, 1895.
Miscellaneous Studies. Ed. C. L. Shadwell, 1895.
Gaston de Latour. Ed. C. L. Shadwell, 1896.

COLLECTED EDITIONS

Works. 1901. Includes the above plus *Essays from the Guardian.*
Works. 1910. New Library Edition, reprinted 1967.

SELECTED CRITICISM

Benson, A. C. *Walter Pater.* 1906.
Cecil, Lord David. *Walter Pater, the Scholar Artist.* Cambridge, 1955.
Child, R. C. *The Aesthetic of Pater.* New York, 1946.
Eliot, T. S. 'The Place of Pater.' *The Eighteen Eighties.* Ed. De La
Mare, 1930. Reprinted as 'Arnold and Pater' in *Selected Essays.*
Third edition, 1951.
Fletcher, Iain. *Walter Pater.* 1959.
d'Hangest, Germain. *Walter Pater.* Paris, 1961.
Hough, Graham. *The Last Romantics.* 1949.
Johnson, R. V. *A Study of Walter Pater's Critical Outlook and Achievement.*
Melbourne, 1961.
de Laura, D. J. *Hebrew and Hellene in Victorian England.* Austin, 1969.
More, P. E. *The Drift of Romanticism.* 1913.
Ward, Anthony. *Walter Pater, The Idea in Nature.* 1966.
Wellek, René. *A History of Modern Criticism, 1750–1950.* Vol. 3. 1958.
Young, Helen. *The Writings of Walter Pater.* Bryn Mawr, 1933.

Unless otherwise stated the place of publication is London.

Texts

'Coleridge's Writings.' *Westminster Review*, 1866.
'Winckelmann.' *Westminster Review*, 1866.
'Conclusion.' First edition of *The Renaissance*, 1873.
'Aesthetic Poetry.' First edition of *Appreciations*, 1889.
'A Novel by Mr Oscar Wilde.' *The Bookman*, November 1891.

All other works; New Library Edition, Macmillan, 1910. Reprinted by Blackwell, 1967.

The essays are reprinted in the form in which they appear in the above publications.

The Youthful Ideal of Culture

COLERIDGE'S WRITINGS[1]

Conversations, Letters, and Recollections of S. T. Coleridge
Edited by Thomas Allsop. London: T. Farrah

Forms of intellectual and spiritual culture often exercise their subtlest and most artful charm when life is already passing from them. Searching and irresistible as are the changes of the human spirit on its way to perfection, there is yet so much elasticity of temper that what must pass away sooner or later is not disengaged all at once even from the highest order of minds. <u>Nature, which by one law of development evolves ideas, moralities, modes of inward life, and represses them in turn, has in this way provided that the earlier growth should propel its fibres into the latter, and so transmit the whole of its forces in an unbroken continuity of life</u>. Then comes the spectacle of the reserve of the elder generation exquisitely refined by the antagonism of the new. That current of new life chastens them as they contend against it. Weaker minds do not perceive the change, clearer minds abandon themselves to it. To feel the change everywhere, yet not to abandon oneself to it, is a situation of difficulty and contention. Communicating in this way to the passing stage of culture the charm of what is chastened, high-strung, athletic, they yet detach the highest minds from the past by pressing home its difficulties and finally proving it impossible. Such is the charm of Julian, of St Louis, perhaps of Luther; in the narrower compass of modern times, of Dr Newman and Lacordaire; it is also the peculiar charm of Coleridge.

Modern thought is distinguished from ancient by its cultivation of the 'relative' spirit in place of the 'absolute'. Ancient philosophy sought to arrest every object in an eternal outline, to fix thought in a necessary formula, and types of life in a classification by 'kinds' or genera. To the modern spirit nothing is or can be rightly known except relatively under conditions. [An ancient philosopher indeed started a philosophy of the relative, but only as an enigma. So the germs of almost all <u>philosophical ideas were enfolded in the mind of antiquity</u>, and fecundated one by one in after ages by

[handwritten marginal note:] the relation to the Greek ideal is cardinal — no question here of the relative

the external influences of art, religion, culture in the natural
sciences, belonging to a particular generation which suddenly becomes pre-occupied by a formula or theory, not so much new
as penetrated by a new meaning and expressiveness.] So the
idea of 'the relative' has been fecundated in modern times by the
influence of the sciences of observation. These sciences reveal
types of life evanescing into each other by inexpressible refinements of
change. Things pass into their opposites by accumulation of undefinable quantities. The growth of those sciences consists in a
continual analysis of facts of rough and general observation into
groups of facts more precise and minute. A faculty for truth is a power
of distinguishing and fixing delicate and fugitive details. The moral
world is ever in contact with the physical; the relative spirit has
invaded moral philosophy from the ground of the inductive sciences.
There it has started a new analysis of the relations of body and mind,
good and evil, freedom and necessity. Hard and abstract moralities
are yielding to a more exact estimate of the subtlety and complexity
of our life. Always as an organism increases in perfection the conditions of its life become more complex. Man is the most complex of
the products of nature. Character merges into temperament; the
nervous system refines itself into intellect. His physical organism is
played upon not only by the physical conditions about it, but by
remote laws of inheritance, the vibrations of long past acts reaching
him in the midst of the new order of things in which he lives. When
we have estimated these conditions he is not yet simple and isolated;
for the mind of the race, the character of the age, sway him this way or
that through the medium of language and ideas. It seems as if the
most opposite statements about him were alike true; he is so receptive,
all the influences of the world and of society ceaselessly playing upon
him, so that every hour in his life is unique, changed altogether by a
stray word, or glance, or touch. The truth of these relations experience
gives us; not the truth of eternal outlines effected once for all, but a
world of fine gradations and subtly linked conditions, shifting
intricately as we ourselves change; and bids us by constant clearing
of the organs of observation and perfecting of analysis to make what
we can of these. To the intellect, to the critical spirit, these subtleties
of effect are more precious than anything else. What is lost in precision
of form is gained in intricacy of expression. [To suppose that what
is called 'ontology' is what the speculative instinct seeks is the misconception of a backward school of logicians.] Who would change the
colour or curve of a roseleaf for that οὐσία ἀχρώματος, ἀσχημάτιστος,
ἀναφής. [A transcendentalism that makes what is abstract more
excellent than what is concrete has nothing akin to the leading

philosophies of the world.] The true illustration of the speculative temper is not the Hindoo, lost to sense, understanding, individuality; but such an one as Göthe, to whom every moment of life brought its share of experimental, individual knowledge, by whom no touch of the world of form, colour, and passion was disregarded.

The literary life of Coleridge was a disinterested struggle against the application of the relative spirit to moral and religious questions. Everywhere he is restlessly scheming to apprehend the absolute; to affirm it effectively; to get it acknowledged. Coleridge failed in that attempt, happily even for him, for it was a struggle against the increasing life of the mind itself. The real loss was, that this controversial interest betrayed him into a direction which was not for him the path of the highest intellectual success; a direction in which his artistic talent could never find the conditions of its perfection. Still, there is so much witchery about his poems, that it is as a poet that he will most probably be permanently remembered. How did his choice of a controversial interest, his determination to affirm the absolute, weaken or modify his poetical gift?

In 1798 he joined Wordsworth in the composition of a volume of poems—the 'Lyrical Ballads'. What Wordsworth then wrote is already vibrant with that blithe *élan* which carried him to final happiness and self-possession. In Coleridge we feel already that faintness and obscure dejection which cling like some contagious damp to all his writings. Wordsworth was to be distinguished by a joyful and penetrative conviction of the existence of certain latent affinities between nature and the human mind, which reciprocally gild the mind and nature with a kind of 'heavenly alchemy'.[2]

> ——'My voice proclaims
> How exquisitely the individual mind
> (And the progressive powers perhaps no less
> Of the whole species,) to the external world
> Is fitted:—and how exquisitely, too,
> The external world is fitted to the mind:
> And the creation, by no lower name
> Can it be called, which they with blended might
> Accomplish.'*

In Wordsworth this took the form of an unbroken dreaming over the aspects and transitions of nature, a reflective, but altogether unformulated, analysis of them.

There are in Coleridge's poems expressions of this conviction as

---

* Preface to the 'Excursion'.

deep as Wordsworth's. But Coleridge could never have abandoned himself to the dream as Wordsworth did, because the first condition of such abandonment is an unvexed quietness of heart. No one can read the 'Lines composed above Tintern' without feeling how potent the physical element was among the conditions of Wordsworth's genius:—'felt in the blood and felt along the heart',—'My whole life I have lived in quiet thought'. The stimulus which most artists require from nature he can renounce. He leaves the ready-made glory of the Swiss mountains to reflect a glory on a mouldering leaf. He loves best to watch the floating thistledown, because of its hint at an unseen life in the air. Coleridge's temperament, ἀεί ἐν σφοδρᾷ-ὀρέξει, with its faintness, its grieved dejection, could never have been like that.

> 'My genial spirits fail;
>   And what can these avail
> To lift the smothering weight from off my breast?
>   It were a vain endeavour,
>   Though I should gaze for ever
> On that green light that lingers in the west:
> I may not hope from outward forms to win
> The passion and the life whose fountains are within.'

It is that flawless temperament in Wordsworth which keeps his conviction of a latent intelligence in nature within the limits of sentiment or instinct, and confines it to those delicate and subdued shades of expression which perfect art allows. In sadder dispositions, that is in the majority of cases, where such a conviction has existed, it has stiffened into a formula, it has frozen into a scientific or pseudo-scientific theory. For the perception of those affinities brings one so near the absorbing speculative problems of life—optimism, the proportion of man to his place in nature, his prospects in relation to it —that it ever tends to become theory through their contagion. Even in Göthe, who has brilliantly handled the subject in his lyrics entitled 'Gott und Welt', it becomes something stiffer than poetry; it is tempered by the 'pale cast' of his technical knowledge of the nature of colours, of anatomy, of the metamorphosis of plants.

That, however, which had only a limited power of Coleridge as sentiment, entirely possessed him as a philosophical idea. We shall see in what follows how deep its power was, how it pursued him everywhere, and seemed to him to interpret every question. Wordsworth's poetry is an optimism; it says man's relation to the world is, and may be seen by man to be, a perfect relation; but it is an optimism that begins and ends in an abiding instinct. Coleridge accepts the same optimism as a philosophical idea, but an idea is relative to an intellectual assent; sometimes it seems a better expression of facts, sometimes a worse, as the understanding weighs it in the logical balances. And so it is not a permanent consolation. It is only in the rarer moments of intellectual warmth and sunlight that it is entirely credible. In less exhilarating moments that perfect relation of man and nature seems to shift and fail; that is, the philosophical idea ceases to be realizable; and with Coleridge its place is not supplied, as with Wordsworth, by the corresponding sentiment or instinct.

What in Wordsworth is a sentiment or instinct, is in Coleridge a philosophical idea. In other words, Coleridge's talent is a more intellectual one than Wordsworth's, more dramatic, more self-conscious. Wordsworth's talent, deeply reflective as it is, because its base is an instinct, is deficient in self-knowledge. Possessed by the rumours and voices of the haunted country, the borders of which he has passed alone, he never thinks of withdrawing from it to look down upon it from one of the central heights of human life. His power absorbs him, not he it; he cannot turn it round or get without it; he does not estimate its general relation to life. But Coleridge, just because the essence of his talent is the intuition of an idea, commands his talent. He not only feels with Wordsworth the expression of mind in nature, but he can project that feeling outside him, reduce it to a psychological law, define its relation to other elements of culture, place it in a complete view of life.

And in some such activity as that, varied as his wide learning, in a many-sided dramatic kind of poetry, assigning its place and value to every mode of the inward life, seems to have been for Coleridge the original path of artistic success. But in order to follow that path one must hold ideas loosely in the relative spirit, not seek to stereotype any one of the many modes of that life; one must acknowledge that the mind is ever greater than its own products, devote ideas to the service of art rather than of γνῶσις, not disquiet oneself about the absolute. Perhaps Coleridge is more interesting because he did not follow this path. Repressing his artistic interest and voluntarily discolouring his own work, he turned to console and strengthen the human mind, vulgarized or dejected, as he believed, by the acquisition of new knowledge about itself in the '*éclaircissement*' of the eighteenth century.

What the reader of our own generation will least find in Coleridge's prose writings is the excitement of the literary sense. And yet in those grey volumes we have the production of one who made way ever by a charm, the charm of voice, of aspect, of language, above all, by the intellectual charm of new, moving, luminous ideas. Perhaps the chief

offence in Coleridge is an excess of seriousness, a seriousness that arises
not from any moral principle, but from a misconception of the perfect
manner. There is a certain shade of levity and unconcern, the perfect
manner of the eighteenth century, which marks complete culture in
the handling of abstract questions. The humanist, he who possesses
that complete culture, does not weep over the failure of a theory of
the quantification of the predicate, nor shriek over the fall of a
philosophical formula. A kind of humour is one of the conditions of
the true mental attitude in the criticism of past stages of thought.
Humanity cannot afford to be too serious about them, any more than
a man of good sense can afford to be too serious in looking back upon
his own childhood. Plato, whom Coleridge claims as the first of his
spiritual ancestors, Plato, as we remember him, [a true humanist,
with Petrarch and Göthe and M. Renan,] holds his theories lightly,
glances with a blithe and naïve inconsequence from one view to
another, not anticipating the burden of meaning 'views' will one day
have for humanity. In reading him one feels how lately it was that
Crœsus thought it a paradox to say that external prosperity was not
necessarily happiness.[3] But on Coleridge lies the whole weight of the
sad reflection that has since come into the world, with which for us
the air is full, which the children in the market-place repeat to each
other. Even his language is forced and broken, lest some saving
formula should be lost—distinctities, enucleation, pentad of operative
Christianity—he has a whole vocabulary of such phrases, and expects
to turn the tide of human thought by fixing the sense of such expressions as reason, understanding, idea.

Again, he has not the jealousy of the true artist in excluding all
associations that have no charm or colour or gladness in them; everywhere he allows the impress of an inferior theological literature; [he
is often prolix and importunate about most indifferent heroes—Sir
Alexander Ball, Dr Bell, even Dr Bowyer, the coarse pedant of the
Blue-coat School. And the source of all this is closely connected with
the source of his literary activity. For Coleridge had chosen as the
mark of his literary egotism a kind of intellectual *tour de force*—to
found a religious philosophy, to do something with the idea in spite
of the essential nature of the idea. And therefore all is fictitious from
the beginning. He had determined, that which is humdrum, insipid,
which the human spirit has done with, shall yet stimulate and inspire.
What he produced symbolizes this purpose—the mass of it *ennuyant*,
depressing: the 'Aids to Reflection', for instance, with Archbishop
Leighton's vague pieties all twisted into the jargon of a spiritualistic
philosophy. But sometimes 'the pulse of the God's blood' does
transmute it, kindling here and there a spot that begins to live; as in

that beautiful fragment at the end of the 'Church and State',* or in the distilled and concentrated beauty of such a passage as this,—

'The first range of hills, that encircles the scanty vale of human life, is the horizon for the majority of its inhabitants. On its ridges the common sun is born and departs. From them the stars rise, and touching them they vanish. By the many, even this range, the natural limit and bulwark of the vale, is but imperfectly known. Its higher ascents are too often hidden by mists and clouds from uncultivated swamps, which few have courage or curiosity to penetrate. To the multitude below these vapours appear now as the dark haunts of terrific agents, on which none may intrude with impunity; and now all a-glow, with colours not their own, they are gazed at as the splendid palaces of happiness and power. But in all ages there have been a few who, measuring and sounding the rivers of the vale at the feet of their furthest inaccessible falls, have learned that the sources must be far higher and far inward; a few who, even in the level streams, have detected elements which neither the vale itself nor the surrounding mountains contained or could supply.'—Biographia Literaria, vol. I. p. 247.

'I was driven from life in motion to life in thought and sensation.' So Coleridge sums up his childhood with its delicacy, its sensitiveness, and passion. From his tenth to his eighteenth year he was at a rough school in London. Speaking of this time, he says:—

'When I was first plucked up and transplanted from my birthplace and family, Providence, it has often occurred to me, gave me the first intimation that it was my lot, and that it was best for me, to make or find my way of life a detached individual, a *terræ filius*, who was to ask love or service of no one on any more specific relation than that of being a man, and as such to take my chance for the free charities of humanity.'†

Even his fine external nature was for years repressed, wronged, driven inward—'at fourteen I was in a continual state of low fever'. He becomes a dreamer, an eager student, but without ambition.

This depressed boy is nevertheless, on the spiritual side, the child of a noble house. At twenty-five he is exercising a wonderful charm, and has defined for himself a peculiar line of intellectual activity. He had left Cambridge without a degree, a Unitarian. Unable to take orders, he determined through Southey's influence to devote himself to literature. When he left Cambridge there was a prejudice against him which has given occasion to certain suspicions. Those who knew

* Page 208.
† Biographical Supplement to Biographia Literaria, chap ii.

him best discredit these suspicions. What is certain is that he was subject to fits of violent, sometimes fantastic, despondency. He retired to Stowey, in Somersetshire, to study poetry and philosophy. In 1797 his poetical gift was in full flower; he wrote 'Kubla Khan', the first part of 'Christabel', and the 'Ancient Mariner'. His literary success grew in spite of opposition. He had a strange attractive gift of conversation, or rather of monologue, as De Stael said, full of *bizarrerie*, with the rapid alternations of a dream, and here and there a sudden summons into a world strange to the hearer, abounding with images drawn from a sort of divided, imperfect life, as of one to whom the external world penetrated only in part, and blended with all this passages of the deepest obscurity, precious only for their musical cadence, the echo in Coleridge of the eloquence of the older English writers, of whom he was so ardent a lover. All through this brilliant course we may discern the power of the Asiatic [4] temperament, of that voluptuousness which is perhaps connected with his appreciation of the intimacy, the almost mystical *rapport* between man and nature. 'I am much better', he writes, 'and my new and tender health is all over me like a voluptuous feeling'.

And whatever fame, or charm, or life-inspiring gift he has had is the vibration of the interest he excited then, the propulsion into years that clouded his early promise of that first buoyant, irresistible self-assertion: so great is even the indirect power of a sincere effort towards the ideal life, of even a temporary escape of the spirit from routine. [Perhaps, the surest sign of his election—that he was indeed, on the spiritual side, the child of a noble house—is that story of the Pantisocratic scheme, which at this distance looks so grotesque. In his enthusiasm for the French Revolution, the old communistic dream with its appeal to nature (perhaps a little theatrical), touched him, as it had touched Rousseau, Saint-Pierre, and Chateaubriand. He had married one, his affection for whom seems to have been only a passing feeling; with her and a few friends he was to found a communistic settlement on the banks of the Susquehannah—'the name was pretty and metrical'. It was one of Coleridge's lightest dreams; but also one which could only have passed through the liberal air of his earlier life. The later years of the French Revolution, which for us have discredited all such dreams, deprived him of that youthfulness which is the preservative element in a literary talent.]

In 1798, he visited Germany. A beautiful fragment of this period remains, describing a spring excursion to the Brocken. His excitement still vibrates in it. Love, all joyful states of mind, are self-expressive; they loosen the tongue, they fill the thoughts with sensuous images, they harmonize one with the world of sight. We hear of the 'rich graciousness and courtesy' of Coleridge's manner, of the white and delicate skin, the abundant black hair, the full, almost animal lips, that whole physiognomy of the dreamer already touched with fanaticism. One says of the text of one of his Unitarian sermons, 'his voice rose like a stream of rich distilled perfumes'; another, 'he talks like an angel, and does—nothing'.

[Meantime, he had designed an intellectual novelty in the shape of a religious philosophy. Socinian theology and the philosophy of Hartley had become distasteful. 'Whatever is against right reason, that no faith can oblige us to believe.' Coleridge quotes these words from Jeremy Taylor. And yet ever since the dawn of the Renaissance, had subsisted a conflict between reason and faith. From the first, indeed, the Christian religion had affirmed the existence of such a conflict, and had even based its plea upon its own weakness in it. In face of the classical culture, with its deep wide-struck roots in the world as it permanently exists, St Paul asserted the claims of that which could not appeal with success to any genuinely human principle. Paradox as it was, that was the strength of the new spirit; for how much is there at all times in humanity which cannot appeal with success for encouragement or tolerance to any genuinely human principle. In the Middle Ages it might seem that faith had reconciled itself to philosophy; the Catholic church was the leader of the world's life as well as of the spirit's. Looking closer we see that the conflict is still latent there; the supremacy of faith is only a part of the worship of sorrow and weakness which marks the age. The weak are no longer merely a majority, they are all Europe. It is not that faith has become one with reason; but a strange winter, a strange suspension of life, has passed over the classical culture which is only the human reason in its most trenchant form. Glimpse after glimpse, as that pagan culture awoke to life the conflict was felt once more. It is at the court of Frederick II that the Renaissance first becomes discernible as an actual power in European society. How definite and unmistakable is the attitude of faith towards that! Ever since the Reformation all phases of theology had been imperfect philosophies, reluctant philosophies—that is, in which there was a religious *arrière pensée*; philosophies which could never be in the ascendant in a sincerely scientific sphere. The two elements had never really mixed. Writers so different as Locke and Taylor have each his liberal philosophy, and each has his defence of the orthodox belief; but, also, each has a divided mind: we wonder how the two elements could have existed side by side; brought together in a single mind, but unable to fuse in it, they reveal their radical contrariety. The Catholic church and

humanity are two powers that divide the intellect and spirit of man.[5]
On the Catholic side is faith, rigidly logical as Ultramontanism, with
a proportion of the facts of life, that is, all that is despairing in life
coming naturally under its formula. On the side of humanity is all
that is desirable in the world, all that is sympathetic with its laws,
and succeeds through that sympathy. Doubtless, for the individual,
there are a thousand intermediate shades of opinion, a thousand
resting-places for the religious spirit; still, τὸ διορίζειν οὐκ ἔστι τῶν
πολλῶν, fine distinctions are not for the majority; and this makes
time eventually a dogmatist, working out the opposition in its most
trenchant form, and fixing the horns of the dilemma; until, in the
present day, we have on one side Pius IX., the true descendant of the
fisherman, issuing the Encyclical, pleading the old promise against
the world with a special kind of justice; and on the other side, the
irresistible modern culture, which, as religious men often remind us,
is only Christian accidentally.

The peculiar temper of Coleridge's intellect made the idea of
reconciling this conflict very seductive. With a true speculative talent
he united a false kind of subtlety and the full share of vanity. A
dexterous intellectual *tour de force* has always an independent charm;
and therefore it is well for the cause of truth that the directness,
sincerity, and naturalness of things are beyond a certain limit
sacrificed in vain to a factitious interest. A method so forced as that of
Coleridge's religious philosophy is from the first doomed to be
insipid, so soon as the temporary interest or taste or curiosity it was
designed to meet has passed away.] Then, as to the manner of such
books as the 'Aids to Reflection', or 'The Friend':—These books
came from one whose vocation was in the world of art; and yet,
perhaps, of all books that have been influential in modern times, they
are farthest from the classical form—bundles of notes—the original
matter inseparably mixed up with that borrowed from others—the
whole just that mere preparation for an artistic effect which the
finished artist would be careful one day to destroy. Here, again, we
have a trait profoundly characteristic of Coleridge. He often attempts
to reduce a phase of thought subtle and exquisite to conditions too
rough for it. He uses a purely speculative gift in direct moral edifica-
tion. Scientific truth is something fugitive, relative, full of fine
gradations; he tries to fix it in absolute formulas. The 'Aids to Reflection', or 'The Friend', is an effort to propagate the volatile spirit of
conversation into the less ethereal fabric of a written book; and it is
only here that the poorer matter becomes vibrant, is really lifted by
the spirit.

At forty-two, we find Coleridge saying, in a letter:—

'I feel with an intensity unfathomable by words my utter nothingness, impotence, and worthlessness in and for myself. I have learned what a sin is against an infinite, imperishable being such as is the soul of man. The consolations, at least the sensible sweetness of hope, I do not possess. On the contrary, the temptation which I have constantly to fight up against is a fear that, if annihilation and the possibility of heaven were offered to my choice, I should choose the former'.*

What was the cause of this change? That is precisely the point on which, after all the gossip there has been, we are still ignorant. At times Coleridge's opium excesses were great; but what led to those excesses must not be left out of account. From boyhood he had a tendency to low fever, betrayed by his constant appetite for bathing and swimming, which he indulged even when a physician had opposed it. In 1803, he went to Malta as secretary to the English Governor. His daughter suspects that the source of the evil was there, that for one of his constitution the climate of Malta was deadly. At all events, when he returned, the charm of those five wonderful years had failed at the source.

De Quincey said of him, 'he wanted better bread than can be made with wheat'. Lamb said of him that from boyhood he had 'hungered for eternity'. Henceforth those are the two notes of his life. From this time we must look for no more true literary talent in him. His style becomes greyer and greyer, his thoughts *outré*, exaggerated, a kind of credulity or superstition exercised upon abstract words. Like Clifford, in Hawthorne's beautiful romance—the born Epicurean, who by some strange wrong has passed the best of his days in a prison—he is the victim of a division of the will, often showing itself in trivial things: he could never chooose on which side of the garden path he would walk. In 1803, he wrote a poem on 'The Pains of Sleep'. That unrest increased. Mr Gillman tells us 'he had long been greatly afflicted with nightmare, and when residing with us was frequently aroused from his painful sleep by any one of the family who might hear him'.

That faintness and continual dissolution had its own consumptive refinements, and even brought as to the 'Beautiful Soul', in 'Wilhelm Meister', a faint religious ecstasy—that singing in the sails which is not of the breeze. Here, again, is a note of Coleridge's:—

'In looking at objects of nature while I am thinking, as at yonder moon, dim-glimmering through the window-pane, I seem rather to be seeking, as it were asking, a symbolical language for something within me that already and for ever exists, than observing anything new. Even when that latter is

* Quoted in Gillman's 'Life of Coleridge'.

the case, yet still I have always an obscure feeling, as if that new phenomenon were the dim awaking of a forgotten or hidden truth of my inner nature.' Then, 'while I was preparing the pen to write this remark, I lost the train of thought which had led me to it'.

What a distemper of the eye of the mind! What an almost bodily distemper there is in that!

Coleridge's intellectual sorrows were many; but he had one singular intellectual happiness. With an inborn-taste for transcendental philosophy, he lived just at the time when that philosophy took an immense spring in Germany, and connected itself with a brilliant literary movement. He had the luck to light upon it in its freshness, and introduce it to his countrymen. What an opportunity for one reared on the colourless English philosophies, but who feels an irresistible attraction towards metaphysical synthesis! How rare are such occasions of intellectual contentment! This transcendental philosophy, chiefly as systematized by Schelling, Coleridge applies with an eager, unwearied subtlety, to the questions of theology and art-criticism. It is in his theory of art-criticism that he comes nearest to true and important principles; that is the least fugitive part of his work. Let us take this first; here we shall most clearly apprehend his main principle.

What, then, is the essence of this criticism? On the whole it may be described as an attempt to reclaim the world of art as a world of fixed laws—to show that the creative activity of genius and the simplest act of thought are but higher and lower products of the laws of a universal logic. Criticism, feeling its own unsuccess in dealing with the greater works of art, has sometimes made too much of those dark and capricious suggestions of genius which even the intellect possessed by them is unable to track or recal. It has seemed due to their half-sacred character to look for no link between the process by which they were produced and the slighter processes of the mind. Coleridge assumes that the highest phases of thought must be more, not less, than the lower subjects of law.

With this interest, in the 'Biographia Literaria', he refines Schelling's 'Philosophy of Nature' into a theory of art. 'Es giebt kein Plagiat in der Philosophie', says Heine, alluding to the charge brought against Schelling of unacknowledged borrowing from Bruno;* and certainly that which is common to Coleridge and Schelling is of far earlier origin than the Renaissance. Schellingism, the 'Philosophy of Nature', is indeed a constant tradition in the history of thought; it embodies a permanent type of the speculative temper. That mode of

* 'Zur Geschichte der Religion und Philosophie in Deutschland,' buch 3.

conceiving nature as a mirror or reflex of the intelligence of man may be traced up to the first beginnings of Greek speculation. There are two ways of envisaging those aspects of nature which appear to bear the impress of reason or intelligence. There is the deist's way, which regards them merely as marks of design, which separates the informing mind from nature as the mechanist from the machine; and there is the pantheistic way, which identifies the two, which regards nature itself as the living energy of an intelligence of the same kind as, but vaster than, the human. Greek philosophy, finding indications of mind everywhere, dwelling exclusively in its observations on that which is general or formal, on that which modern criticism regards as the modification of things by the mind of the observer, adopts the latter, or pantheistic way, through the influence of the previous mythological period. Mythology begins in the early necessities of language, of which it is a kind of accident. But at a later period its essence changes; it becomes what it was not at its birth, the servant of a genuine poetic interest, a kind of *vivification* of nature. Played upon by those accidents of language, the Greek mind becomes possessed by the conception of nature as living, thinking, almost speaking to the mind of man. This unfixed poetical prepossession reduced to an abstract form, petrified into an idea, is the conception which gives a unity of aim to Greek philosophy. Step by step it works out the substance of the Hegelian formula : ' Was ist, das ist vernunftig; was vernunftig ist, das ist'—Whatever is, is according to reason; whatever is according to reason, that is. A science of which that could be the formula is still but an intellectual aspiration; the formula of true science is different. Experience, which has gradually saddened the earth's colour, stiffened its motions, withdrawn from it some blithe and debonair presence, has moderated our demands upon science. The positive method makes very little account of marks of intelligence in nature; in its wider view of phenomena it sees that those incidents are a minority, and may rank as happy coincidences; it absorbs them in the simpler conception of law. But the suspicion of a mind latent in nature, struggling for release and intercourse with the intellect of man through true ideas, has never ceased to haunt a certain class of minds. Started again and again in successive periods by enthusiasts on the antique pattern, in each case the thought has seemed paler and more evanescent amidst the growing consistency and sharpness of outline of other and more positive forms of knowledge. Still, wherever a speculative instinct has been united with extreme inwardness of temperament, as in Jakob Böhme, there the old Greek conception, like some seed floating in the air, has taken root and sprung up anew. Coleridge, thrust inward upon himself, driven from 'life in thought

and sensation' to life in thought only, feels in that dark London school
a thread of the Greek mind vibrating strangely in him. At fifteen he is
discoursing on Plotinus, and has translated the hymns of Synesius.
So in later years he reflects from Schelling the flitting tradition. He
conceives a subtle co-ordination between the ideas of the mind and
the laws of the natural world. Science is to be attained not by observation, analysis, generalization, but by the evolution or recovery of those
ideas from within by a sort of ἀνάμνησις, every group of observed
facts remaining an enigma until the appropriate idea is struck upon
them from the mind of Newton or Cuvier, the genius in whom
sympathy with the universal reason is entire. Next he supposes that
this reason or intelligence in nature gradually becomes reflective—
self-conscious. He fancies he can track through all the simpler orders
of life fragments of an eloquent prophecy about the human mind. He
regards the whole of nature as a development of higher forms out of
the lower through shade after shade of systematic change. The dim stir
of chemical atoms towards the axes of a crystal form, the trance-like
life of plants, the animal troubled by strange irritabilities, are stages
which anticipate consciousness. All through that increasing stir of
life this was forming itself; each stage in its unsatisfied susceptibilities
seeming to be drawn out of its own limits by the more pronounced
current of life on its confines, the 'shadow of approaching humanity'
gradually deepening, the latent intelligence working to the surface.
At this point the law of development does not lose itself in caprice;
rather it becomes more constraining and incisive. From the lowest
to the highest acts of intelligence there is another range of refining
shades. Gradually the mind concentrates itself, frees itself from the
limits of the particular, the individual, attains a strange power of
modifying and centralizing what it receives from without according
to an inward ideal. At last, in imaginative genius, ideas become
effective; the intelligence of nature, with all its elements connected
and justified, is clearly reflected; and the interpretation of its latent
purposes is fixed in works of art.

[In this fanciful and bizarre attempt to rationalize art, to range it
under the dominion of law, there is still a gap to be filled up. What is
that common law of the mind of which a work of art and the slighter
acts of thought are alike products? Here Coleridge weaves in Kant's
fine-spun theory of the transformation of sense into perception. What
every theory of perception has to explain is that associative power
which gathers isolated sensible qualities into the objects of the world
about us. Sense, without an associative power, would be only a
threadlike stream of colours, sounds, odours—each struck upon one for
a moment and then withdrawn. The basis of this association may be

represented as a material one, a kind of many-coloured 'etching' on
the brain. Hartley has dexterously handled this hypothesis. The charm
of his 'theory of vibrations' is the vivid image it presents to the fancy.
How large an element in a speculative talent is the command of these
happy images! Coleridge, by a finer effort of the same kind, a greater
delicacy of fancy, detects all sorts of slips, transitions, breaks of
continuity in Hartley's glancing cobweb. Coleridge, with Kant,
regards all association as effected by a power within, to which he gives
a fanciful Greek name.* In an act of perception there is the matter
which sense presents, colour, tone, feeling; but also a form or mould,
such as space, unity, causation, suggested from within. In these forms
we arrest and frame the many attributes of sense. It is like that
simple chemical phenomenon where two colourless fluids uniting
reflect a full colour. Neither matter nor form can be perceived asunder,
they unite into the many-coloured image of life. This theory has
not been able to bear a loyal induction. Even if it were true, how little
it would tell us; how it attenuates fact! There, again, the charm is all
in the clear image; the image of the artist combining a few elementary
colours, curves, sounds into a new whole. Well, this power of association, of concentrating many elements of sense in an object of perception, is refined and deepened into the creative acts of imagination.

We of the modern ages have become so familiarized with the
greater works of art that we are little sensitive of the act of creation in
them; they do not impress us as a new presence in the world. Only
sometimes in productions which realize immediately a profound
emotion and enforce a change in taste, such as 'Werther' or 'Emile',
we are actual witnesses of the moulding of an unforeseen type by some
new principle of association. By imagination, the distinction between
which and fancy is so thrust upon his readers, Coleridge means a
vigorous act of association, which, by simplifying and restraining their
natural expression to an artificial order, refines and perfects the types
of human passion. It represents the excitements of the human mind,
but reflected in a new manner, 'excitement itself imitating order'.
'Originally the offspring of passion', he somewhere says, 'but now
the adopted children of power'. So far there is nothing new or distinctive; every one who can receive from a poem or picture a total
impression will admit so much. What makes the view distinctive in
Coleridge are the Schellingistic associations with which he colours it,
that faint glamour of the philosophy of nature which was ever
influencing his thoughts. That suggested the idea of a subtly winding
parallel, a 'rapport' in every detail, between the human mind and

* Esemplastic, εἰς ἕν πλάττειν.

the world without it, laws of nature being so many transformed ideas. Conversely, the ideas of the human mind would be only transformed laws. Genius would be in a literal sense an exquisitely purged sympathy with nature. Those associative conceptions of the imagination, those unforeseen types of passion, would come not so much of the artifice and invention of the understanding as from self-surrender to the suggestions of nature; they would be evolved by the stir of nature itself realizing the highest reach of its latent intelligence; they would have a kind of antecedent necessity to rise at some time to the surface of the human mind.]

It is natural that Shakspeare should be the idol of all such criticism, whether in England or Germany. The first effect in Shakspeare is that of capricious detail, of the waywardness that plays with the parts careless of the impression of the whole. But beyond there is the constraining unity of effect, the uneffaceable impression of 'Hamlet' or 'Macbeth'. His hand moving freely is curved round by some law of gravitation from within; that is, there is the most constraining unity in the most abundant variety. Coleridge exaggerates this unity into something like the unity of a natural organism, the associative act that effected it into something closely akin to the primitive power of nature itself. 'In the Shakspearian drama', he says, 'there is a vitality which grows and evolves itself from within.' Again,

'He, too, worked in the spirit of nature, by evolving the germ from within by the imaginative power according to the idea. For as the power of seeing is to light, so is an idea in mind to a law in nature. They are correlatives which suppose each other.'

Again,

'The organic form is innate; it shapes, as it developes, itself from within, and the fulness of its development is one and the same with the perfection of its outward form. Such as the life is, such is the form. Nature, the prime genial artist, inexhaustible in diverse powers, is equally inexhaustible in forms; each exterior is the physiognomy of the being within, and even such is the appropriate excellence of Shakspeare, himself a nature humanised, a genial understanding, directing self-consciously a power and an implicit wisdom deeper even than our consciousness.' [6]

There 'the absolute' has been affirmed in the sphere of art; and thought begins to congeal. Coleridge has not only overstrained the elasticity of his hypothesis, but has also obscured the true interest of art. For after all the artist has become something almost mechanical; instead of being the most luminous and self-possessed phase of consciousness, the associative act itself looks like some organic process of assimilation. The work of art is sometimes likened to the living organism. That expresses the impression of a self-delighting, independent life which a finished work of art gives us; it does not express the process by which that work was produced. Here there is no blind ferment of lifeless elements to realize a type. By exquisite <u>analysis</u> the artist attains <u>clearness of idea</u>, then by many stages of <u>refining clearness of expression</u>. He moves slowly over his work, <u>calculating</u> the tenderest tone, and <u>restraining</u> the subtlest curve, never letting his hand or fancy move at large, gradually <u>refining</u> flaccid spaces to the higher degree of <u>expressiveness</u>. Culture, at least, values even in transcendent works of art the power of the understanding in them, their logical process of construction, the spectacle of supreme intellectual dexterity which they afford.

[marginal note: Yet his own work remain so opaque]

Coleridge's criticism may well be remembered as part of the long pleading of German culture for the things '<u>behind the veil</u>'. It recals us from the work of art to the mind of the artist; and after all, this is what is infinitely precious, and the work of art only as the index of it. Still, that is only the narrower side of a complete criticism. Perhaps it is true, as some one says in Lessing's 'Emilie Galotti', that, if Michael Angelo had been born without hands, he would still have been the greatest of artists. But we must admit the truth also of an opposite view: 'In morals as in art', says M. Renan, 'the word is nothing—the fact is everything. The idea which lurks under a picture of Raphael is a slight matter; it is the picture itself only that counts.'

What constitutes an artistic gift is first of all a natural susceptibility to moments of strange excitement, in which the colours freshen upon our threadbare world, and the routine of things about us is broken by a novel and happier <u>synthesis</u>. These are moments into which other minds may be made to enter, but which they cannot originate. This susceptibility is the element of genius in an artistic gift. Secondly, there is what may be called the talent of projection, of <u>throwing</u> these happy moments into an external concrete form—a statue, or play, or picture. That projection is of all degrees of completeness; its facility and transparence are modified by the circumstances of the individual, his culture and his age. When it is perfectly transparent, the work is classical. Compare the power of projection in Mr Browning's 'Sordello', with that power in the 'Sorrows of Werther'. These two elements determine the two chief aims of criticism. First, it has to classify those initiative moments according to the amount of interest excited in them, to estimate their comparative acceptability, their comparative power of giving joy to those who undergo them. Secondly, it has to test, by a study of the artistic product itself, in connexion with the intellectual and spiritual condition of its age, the

[marginal note: But if ① creates an art object surely there will be a regnal diff. between the two. As we only have the product such an analysis may evolve speculation only]

completeness of the projection. These two aims form the positive, or concrete side of criticism; their direction is not towards a metaphysical definition of the universal element in an artistic effort, but towards a subtle gradation of the shades of difference between one artistic gift and another. This side of criticism is infinitely varied; and it is what French culture more often achieves than the German.

Coleridge has not achieved this side in an equal degree with the other; and this want is not supplied by the 'Literary Remains', which contain his studies on Shakspeare. There we have a repetition, not an application, of the absolute formula. Coleridge is like one who sees in a picture only the rules of perspective, and is always trying to simplify even these. Thus: 'Where there is no humour, but only wit, or the like, there is no growth from within.' 'What is beauty?' he asks. 'It is the unity of the manifold, the coalescence of the diverse.' So of Dante:—'There is a total impression of infinity; the wholeness is not in vision or conception, but in an inner feeling of totality and absolute being.' Again, of the 'Paradise Lost':—'It has the totality of the poem as distinguished from the *ab ovo* birth and parentage or straight line of history.'

That exaggerated inwardness is barren. Here, too, Coleridge's thoughts require to be thawed, to be set in motion, He is admirable in the detection, the analysis and statement, of a few of the highest general laws of art-production. But he withdraws us too far from what we can see, hear, and feel. Doubtless, the idea, the intellectual element, is the spirit and life of art. Still, art is the triumph of the senses and the emotions; and the senses and the emotions must not be cheated of their triumph after all. That strange and beautiful psychology which he employs, with its evanescent delicacies, has not sufficient corporeity. Again, one feels that the discussion about Hartley, meeting us in the way, throws a tone of insecurity over the critical theory which it introduces. Its only effect is to win for the terms in which that criticism is expressed the associations of one side in a metaphysical controversy.

The vagueness and fluidity of Coleridge's theological opinions have been exaggerated through an illusion, which has arisen from the occasional form in which they have reached us. Criticism, then, has to methodize and focus them. They may be arranged under three heads: the general principles of supernaturalism, orthodox dogmas, the interpretation of Scripture. With regard to the first and second, Coleridge ranks as a Conservative thinker; but his principles of Scriptural interpretation resemble Lessing's; they entitle him to be regarded as the founder of the modern liberal school of English theology. By supernaturalism is meant the theory of a divine person in immediate communication with the human mind, dealing with it out of that order of nature which includes man's body and his ordinary trains of thought, according to fixed laws, which the theologian sums up in the doctrines of 'grace' and 'sin'. Of this supernaturalism, the 'Aids to Reflection' attempts to give a metaphysical proof. The first necessity of the argument is to prove that religion, with its supposed experiences of grace and sin, and the realities of a world above the world of sense, is the fulfilment of the constitution of every man, or, in the language of the 'philosophy of nature', is part of the 'idea' of man; so that when those experiences are absent all the rest of his nature is unexplained, like some enigmatical fragment, the construction and working of which we cannot surmise. According to Schelling's principle, the explanation of every phase of life is to be sought in that next above it. This axiom is applied to three supposed stages of man's reflective life: Prudence, Morality, Religion. Prudence, by which Coleridge means something like Bentham's 'enlightened principle of self-preservation', is, he says, an inexplicable instinct, a blind motion in the dark, until it is expanded into morality. Morality, again, is but a groundless prepossession until transformed into a religious recognition of a spiritual world, until, as Coleridge says in his rich figurative language, 'like the main feeder into some majestic lake, rich with hidden springs of its own, it flows into and becomes one with the spiritual life'. A spiritual life, then, being the fulfilment of human nature, implied, if we see clearly, in those instincts which enable one to live on from day to day, is part of the 'idea' of man.

The second necessity of the argument is to prove that 'the idea', according to the principle of the 'philosophy of nature', is an infallible index of the actual condition of the world without us. Here Coleridge introduces an analogy:

'In the world, we see everywhere evidences of a unity, which the component parts are so far from explaining, that they necessarily presuppose it as the cause and condition of their existing as those parts, or even of their existing at all. This antecedent unity, or cause and principle of each union, it has, since the time of Bacon and Kepler, been customary to call a law. This crocus for instance; or any other flower the reader may have before his sight, or choose to bring before his fancy; that the root, stem, leaves, petals, &c., cohere to one plant is owing to an antecedent power or principle in the seed which existed before a single particle of the matters that constitute the size and visibility of the crocus had been attracted from the surrounding soil, air, and moisture. Shall we turn to the seed? there, too, the same necessity meets us: an antecedent unity must here, too, be supposed. Analyze the seeds with the finest tools, and let the solar microscope come in aid of your senses, what do you find?—means and instruments; a wondrous fairy tale of nature, magazines of food, stores of various sorts, pipes, spiracles, defences; a house of many chambers, and the owner and inhabitant invisible.'—'Aids to Reflection', p. 68.

Nature, that is, works by what we may call intact ideas. It co-ordinates every part of the crocus to all the other parts; one stage of its growth to the whole process; and having framed its organism to assimilate certain external elements, it does not cheat it of those elements, soil, air, moisture. Well, if the 'idea' of man is to be intact, he must be enveloped in a supernatural world; and nature always works by intact ideas. The spiritual life is the highest development of the idea of man; there must be a supernatural world corresponding to it.

One finds, it is hard to say how many, difficulties in drawing Coleridge's conclusion. To mention only one of them—the argument looks too like the exploded doctrine of final causes. Of course the crocus would not live unless the conditions of its life were supplied. The flower is made for soil, air, moisture, and it has them; just as man's senses are made for a sensible world, and we have the sensible world. But give the flower the power of dreaming, nourish it on its own reveries, put man's wild hunger of heart and susceptibility to *ennui* in it, and what indication of the laws of the world without it would be afforded by its longing to break its bonds?

In theology people are content with analogies, probabilities, with the empty schemes of arguments for which the data are still lacking; arguments, the rejection of which Coleridge tells us implies 'an evil heart of unbelief', but of which we might as truly say that they derive all their consistency from the peculiar atmosphere of the mind which receives them. Such arguments are received in theology because what chains men to a religion is not its claim on their reason, their hopes or fears, but the glow it affords to the world, its 'beau ideal'. Cole-ridge thinks that if we reject the supernatural, the spiritual element in life will evaporate also, that we shall have to accept a life with narrow horizons, without disinterestedness, harshly cut off from the springs of life in the past. But what is this spiritual element? It is the passion for inward perfection with its sorrows, its aspirations, its joy. These mental states are the delicacies of the higher morality of the few, of Augustine, of the author of the 'Imitation', of Francis de Sales; in their essence they are only the permanent characteristics of the higher life. Augustine, or the author of the 'Imitation', agreeably to the culture of their age, had expressed them in the terms of a metaphysical theory, and expanded them into what theologians call the doctrines of grace and sin, the fluctuations of the union of the soul

with its unseen friend. The life of those who are capable of a passion
for perfection still produces the same mental states; but that religious
expression of them is no longer congruous with the culture of the age.[7]
Still, all inward life works itself out in a few simple forms, and culture
cannot go very far before the religious graces reappear in it in a
subtilized intellectual shape. There are aspects of the religious
character which have an artistic worth distinct from their religious
import. Longing, a chastened temper, spiritual joy, are precious
states of mind, not because they are part of man's duty or because
God has commanded them, still less because they are means of obtain-
ing a reward, but because like culture itself they are remote, refined,
intense, existing only by the triumph of a few over a dead world of
routine in which there is no lifting of the soul at all. If there is no other
world, art in its own interest must cherish such characteristics as
beautiful spectacles. Stephen's face, 'like the face of an angel', has
a worth of its own, even if the opened heaven is but a dream.

Our culture, then, is not supreme, our intellectual life is incomplete,
we fail of the intellectual throne, if we have no inward longing, inward
chastening, inward joy. Religious belief, the craving for objects of
belief, may be refined out of our hearts, but they must leave their
sacred perfume, their spiritual sweetness, behind. This law of the
highest intellectual life has sometimes seemed hard to understand.
Those who maintain the claims of the older and narrower forms of
religious life against the claims of culture are often embarrassed at
finding the intellectual life heated through with the very graces to
which they would sacrifice it. How often in the higher class of theological writings—writings which really spring from an original
religious genius, such as those of Dr Newman—does the modern
aspirant to perfect culture seem to find the expression of the inmost
delicacies of his own life, the same yet different! The spiritualities of
the Christian life have often drawn men on little by little into the
broader spiritualities of systems opposed to it—pantheism, or
positivism, or a philosophy of indifference. Many in our own generation, through religion, have become dead to religion. How often do
we have to look for some feature of the ancient religous life, not in a
modern saint, but in a modern artist or philosopher! For those who
have passed out of Christianity, perhaps its most precious souvenir is
the ideal of a transcendental disinterestedness. Where shall we look
for this ideal? In Spinoza; or perhaps in Bentham or in Austin.

Some of those who have wished to save supernaturalism—as, for
instance, Theodore Parker—have rejected more or less entirely the
dogmas of the Church. Coleridge's instinct is truer than theirs; the
two classes of principles are logically connected. It was in defence of

the dogmas of the Church that Coleridge elaborated his unhappy crotchet of the diversity of the reason from the understanding. The weakness of these dogmas had ever been not so much a failure of the authority of Scripture or tradition in their favour, as their conflict with the reason that they were words rather than conceptions. That analysis of words and conceptions which in modern philosophy has been a principle of continual rejuvenescence with Descartes and Berkeley, as well as with Bacon and Locke, had desolated the field of scholastic theology. It is the rationality of the dogmas of that theology that Coleridge had a taste for proving.

Of course they conflicted with the understanding, with the common daylight of the mind, but then might there not be some mental faculty higher than the understanding? The history of philosophy supplied many authorities for this opinion. Then, according to the 'philosophy of nature', science and art are both grounded upon the 'ideas' of genius, which are a kind of intuition, which are their own evidence. Again, this philosophy was always saying the ideas of the mind must be true, must correspond to reality; and what an aid to faith is that, if one is not too nice in distinguishing between ideas and mere convictions, or prejudices, or habitual views, or safe opinions! Kant also had made a distinction between the reason and the understanding. True, this harsh division of mental faculties is exactly what is most sterile in Kant, the essential tendency of the German school of thought being to show that the mind always acts *en masse*. Kant had defined two senses of reason as opposed to the understanding. First, there was the 'speculative reason', with its 'three categories of totality', God, the soul, and the universe—three mental forms which might give a sort of unity to science, but to which no actual intuition corresponded. The tendency of this part of Kant's critique is to destroy the rational groundwork of theism. Then there was the 'practical reason', on the relation of which to the 'speculative', we may listen to Heinrich Heine:—

'After the tragedy comes the farce. (The tragedy is Kant's destructive criticism of the speculative reason.) So far Immanuel Kant has been playing the relentless philosopher; he has laid siege to heaven.' Heine goes on with some violence to describe the havoc Kant has made of the orthodox belief— 'Old Lampe,* with the umbrella under his arm, stands looking on much disturbed, perspiration and tears of sorrow running down his cheeks. Then Immanuel Kant grows pitiful, and shows that he is not only a great philosopher but also a good man. He considers a little; and then, half in good nature, half in irony, he says, "Old Lampe must have a god, otherwise the poor man will not be happy; but man ought to be happy in this life, the

* The servant who attended Kant in his walks.

practical reason says that; let the practical reason stand surety for the existence of a god; it is all the same to me." Following this argument, Kant distinguishes between the theoretical and the practical reason, and, with the practical reason for a magic wand, he brings to life the dead body of deism, which the theoretical reason had slain.'

Coleridge first confused the speculative reason with the practical, and then exaggerated the variety and the sphere of their combined functions. Then he has given no consistent definition of the reason. It is 'the power of universal and necessary convictions'; it is 'the knowledge of the laws of the whole considered as one'; it is 'the science of all as a whole'. Again, the understanding is 'the faculty judging according to sense', or 'the faculty of means to mediate ends'; and so on. The conception floating in his mind seems to have been a really valuable one; that, namely, of a distinction between an organ of adequate and an organ of inadequate ideas. But when we find him casting about for a definition, not precisely determining the functions of the reason, making long preparations for the 'deduction' of the faculty, as in the third volume of 'The Friend', but never actually starting, we suspect that the reason is a discovery in psychology which Coleridge has a good will to make, and that is all; that he has got no farther than the old vague desire to escape from the limitations of thought by some extraordinary mystical faculty. Some of the clergy eagerly welcomed the supposed discovery. In their difficulties they had often appealed in the old simple way to sentiment and emotion as of higher authority than the understanding, and on the whole had had to get on with very little philosophy. Like M. Jourdain, they were amazed to find that they had been all the time appealing to the reason; now they might actually go out to meet the enemy. Orthodoxy might be cured by a hair of the dog that had bitten it.

Theology is a great house, scored all over with hieroglyphics by perished hands. When we decypher one of those hieroglyphics, we find in it the statement of a mistaken opinion; but knowledge has crept onward since the hand dropped from the wall; we no longer entertain the opinion, and we can trace the origin of the mistake. Dogmas are precious as memorials of a class of sincere and beautiful spirits, who in a past age of humanity struggled with many tears, if not for true knowledge, yet for a noble and elevated happiness. That struggle is the substance, the dogma only its shadowy expression; received traditionally in an altered age, it is the shadow of a shadow, a mere τρίτον εἴδωλον, twice removed from substance and reality. The true method then in the treatment of dogmatic theology must be historical. Englishmen are gradually finding out how much that method has done since the beginning of modern criticism by the hands of such writers as Baur. Coleridge had many of the elements of this method: learning, inwardness, a subtle psychology, a dramatic power of sympathy with modes of thought other than his own. Often in carrying out his own method he gives the true historical origin of a dogma, but with a strange dulness of the historical sense, he regards this as a reason for the existence of the dogma now, not merely as reason for its having existed in the past. Those historical elements he could not envisage in the historical method, because this method is only one of the applications, the most fruitful of them all, of the relative spirit.

After Coleridge's death, seven letters of his on the inspiration of Scripture were published, under the title of 'Confessions of an Inquiring Spirit'. This little book has done more than any other of Coleridge's writings to discredit his name with the orthodox. The frequent occurrence in it of the word 'bibliolatry', borrowed from Lessing, would sufficiently account for this pious hatred. From bibliolatry Coleridge was saved by the spiritualism, which, in questions less simple than that of the infallibility of Scripture, was so retarding to his culture. Bibliolators may remember that one who committed a kind of intellectual suicide by catching at any appearance of a fixed and absolute authority, never dreamed of resting on the authority of a book. His Schellingistic notion of the possibility of absolute knowledge, of knowing God, of a light within every man which might discover to him the doctrines of Christianity, tended to depreciate historical testimony, perhaps historical realism altogether. Scripture is a legitimate sphere for the understanding. He says, indeed, that there is more in the Bible that 'finds' him than he has experienced in all other books put together. But still, 'There is a Light higher than all, even the Word that was in the beginning. If between this Word and the written letter I shall anywhere seem to myself to find a discrepance, I will not conclude that such there actually is; nor on the other hand will I fall under the condemnation of them that would lie for God, but seek as I may, be thankful for what I have—and wait.' Coleridge is the inaugurator of that *via media* of Scriptural criticism which makes much of saving the word 'inspiration', while it attenuates its meaning; which supposes a sort of modified inspiration residing in the whole, not in the several parts. 'The Scriptures were not dictated by an infallible intelligence'; nor 'the writers each and all divinely informed as well as inspired'. 'They refer to other documents, and in all points express themselves as sober-minded and veracious writers under ordinary circumstances are known to do.' To make the Bible itself 'the subject of a special article of faith, is an unnecessary and useless abstraction'.

His judgment on the popular view of inspiration is severe. It is borrowed from the Cabbalists; it 'petrifies at once the whole body of Holy Writ, with all its harmonies and symmetrical gradations;—turns it at once into a colossal Memnon's head, a hollow passage for a voice, a voice that mocks the voices of many men, and speaks in their names, and yet is but one voice and the same;—and no man uttered it and never in a human heart was it conceived'. He presses very hard on the tricks of the 'routiniers of desk and pulpit'; forced and fantastic interpretations; 'the strange—in all other writings un-exampled—practice of bringing together into logical dependency detached sentences from books composed at the distance of centuries, nay, sometimes a millennium, from each other, under different dispensations, and for different objects'.

Certainly he is much farther from bibliolatry than from the perfect freedom of the humanist interpreters. Still he has not freed himself from the notion of a sacred canon; he cannot regard the books of Scripture simply as fruits of the human spirit; his criticism is not entirely disinterested. The difficulties he finds are chiefly the supposed immoralities of Scripture; just those difficulties which fade away before the modern or relative spirit, which in the moral world as in the physical traces everywhere change, growth, development. Of historical difficulties, of those deeper moral difficulties which arise for instance from a consideration of the constitutional unveracity of the Oriental mind, he has no suspicion. He thinks that no book of the New Testament was composed so late as A.D. 120.

Coleridge's undeveloped opinions would be hardly worth stating except for the warning they afford against retarding compromises. In reading these letters one never doubts what Coleridge tells us of himself: 'that he loved truth with an indescribable awe', or, as he beautifully says, 'that he would creep towards the light, even if the light had made its way through a rent in the wall of the temple'. And yet there is something sad in reading them by the light which twenty-five years have thrown back upon them. Taken as a whole, they contain a fallacy which a very ardent lover of truth might have detected.

The Bible is not to judge the spirit, but the spirit the Bible. The Bible is to be treated as a literary product. Well, but that is a con-ditional, not an absolute principle—that is not, if we regard it sincerely, a delivery of judgment, but only a suspension of it. If we are true to the spirit of that, we must wait patiently the complete result of modern criticism. Coleridge states that the authority of Scripture is on its trial—that at present it is not known to be an absolute resting-place; and then, instead of leaving that to aid in the formation of a fearless spirit, the spirit which, for instance, would accept the results of M. Renan's investigations, he turns it into a false security by anticipating the judgment of an undeveloped criticism. Twenty-five years of that criticism have gone by, and have hardly verified the anticipation.

The man of science asks, Are absolute principles attainable? What are the limits of knowledge? The answer he receives from science itself is not ambiguous. What the moralist asks is, Shall we gain or lose by surrendering human life to the relative spirit? Experience answers, that the dominant tendency of life is to turn ascertained truth into a dead letter—to make us all the phlegmatic servants of routine. The relative spirit, by dwelling constantly on the more fugitive conditions or circumstances of things, breaking through a thousand rough and brutal classifications, and giving elasticity to inflexible principles, begets an intellectual finesse, of which the ethical result is a delicate and tender justness in the criticism of human life. Who would gain more than Coleridge by criticism in such a spirit? We know how his life has appeared when judged by absolute standards. We see him trying to apprehend the absolute, to stereotype one form of faith, to attain, as he says, 'fixed principles' in politics, morals, and religion; to fix one mode of life as the essence of life, refusing to see the parts as parts only; and all the time his own pathetic history pleads for a more elastic moral philosophy than his, and cries out against every formula less living and flexible than life itself.

'From his childhood he hungered for eternity.' After all, that is the incontestable claim of Coleridge. The perfect flower of any elementary type of life must always be precious to humanity, and Coleridge is the perfect flower of the romantic type. More than Childe Harold, more than Werther, more than René, Coleridge, by what he did, what he was, and what he failed to do, represents that inexhaustible discontent, languor, and home-sickness, the chords of which ring all through our modern literature. Criticism may still discuss the claims of classical and romantic art, or literature, or sentiment; and perhaps one day we may come to forget the horizon, with full knowledge to be content with what is here and now; and that is the essence of classical feeling. But by us of the present moment, by us for whom the Greek spirit, with its engaging naturalness, simple, chastened, debonair, τρυφῆς, ἀβρότητος, χλιδῆς, χαρίτων, ἱμέρου, πόθου πατήρ, is itself the Sangraal of an endless pilgrimage, Coleridge, with his passion for the absolute, for something fixed where all is moving, his faintness, his broken memory, his intellectual disquiet, may still be ranked among the interpreters of one of the constituent elements of our life.

WINCKELMANN[1]

... In one of the *stanze* of the Vatican Raphael has commemorated the tradition of the Catholic religion. Along a strip of infinitely quiet sky, broken in upon by the beatific vision, are ranged the great personages of Christian history, with the Sacrament in the midst. The companion fresco presents a very different company, Dante only appearing in both. Surrounded by the muses of Greek mythology, under a thicket of myrtles, sits Apollo, with the sources of Castalia at his feet. On either side are grouped those on whom the spirit of Apollo descended, the classical and Renaissance poets, to whom the waters of Castalia come down, a river making glad this other city of God. In this fresco it is the classical tradition, the orthodoxy of taste, that Raphael commemorates. Winckelmann's intellectual history authenticates the claims of this tradition in human culture. In the countries where that tradition arose, where it still lurked about its own artistic relics, and changes of language had not broken its continuity, national pride might often light up anew an enthusiasm for it. Aliens might imitate that enthusiasm, and classicism become from time to time an intellectual fashion; but Winckelmann was not farther removed by language than by local aspects and associations from the vestiges of the classical spirit, and he lived at a time when, in Germany, classical studies were out of fashion. Yet, remote in time and place, he feels after the Hellenic world, divines the veins of ancient art, in which its life still circulates, and, like Scyles in the beautiful story of Herodotus, is irresistibly attracted by it. This testimony to the authority of the Hellenic tradition, its fitness to satisfy some vital requirement of the intellect, which Winckelmann contributes as a solitary man of genius, is offered also by the general history of culture. The spiritual forces of the past, which have prompted and informed the culture of a succeeding age, live, indeed, within that culture, but with an absorbed, underground life. The Hellenic element alone has not been so absorbed or content with this underground life; from time to time it has started to the surface; culture has been drawn

27

back to its sources to be clarified and corrected. Hellenism is not merely an element in our intellectual life; it is a constant tradition in it.

Again, individual genius works ever under conditions of time and place; its products are coloured by the varying aspects of nature and type of human form and outward manners of life. There is thus an element of change in art; criticism must never for a moment forget that 'the artist is the child of his time'. But besides these conditions of time and place, and independent of them, there is also an element of permanence, a standard of taste which genius confesses. This standard is maintained in a purely intellectual tradition; it acts upon the artist, not as one of the influences of his own age, but by means of the artistic products of the previous generation, which in youth have excited, and at the same time directed into a particular channel, his sense of beauty. The supreme artistic products of each generation thus form a series of elevated points, taking each from each the reflection of a strange light, the source of which is not in the atmosphere around and above them, but in a stage of society remote from ours. This standard takes its rise in Greece at a definite historical period. A tradition for all succeeding generations, it originates in a spontaneous growth out of the influences of Greek society. . . .[2]

. . . It records the first naïve, unperplexed recognition of man by himself; and it is a proof of the high artistic capacity of the Greeks that they apprehended and remained true to these exquisite limitations, yet in spite of them gave to their creations a vital, mobile individuality.*

Heiterkeit, blitheness or repose, and *Allgemeinheit*, generality or breadth, are, then, the supreme characteristics of the Hellenic ideal. But that generality or breadth has nothing in common with the lax observation, the unlearned thought, the flaccid execution which have sometimes claimed superiority in art on the plea of being 'broad' or 'general'. Hellenic breadth and generality come of a culture minute, severe, constantly renewed, rectifying and concentrating its impressions into certain pregnant types. The base of all artistic genius is the power of conceiving humanity in a new, striking, rejoicing way, of putting a happy world of its own creation in place of the meaner world of common days, of generating around itself an atmosphere with a novel power of refraction, selecting, transforming, recombining the images it transmits, according to the choice of the imaginative intellect. In exercising this power, painting and poetry have a choice

---

* Hegel: Æsthetik, Th. 3, Abschnitt 2.

of subject almost unlimited. The range of characters or persons open to them is as various as life itself; no character, however trivial, misshapen, or unlovely, can resist their magic. This is because those arts can accomplish their function in the choice and development of some special situation, which lifts or glorifies a character in itself not poetical. To realize this situation, to define in a chill and empty atmosphere the focus where rays, in themselves pale and impotent, unite and begin to burn, the artist has to employ the most cunning detail, to complicate and refine upon thought and passion a thousand-fold. The poems of Robert Browning supply brilliant examples of this. His poetry is pre-eminently the poetry of situations. The characters themselves are always of secondary importance; often they are characters in themselves of little interest; they seem to come to him by strange accidents from the ends of the world. His gift is shown by the way in which he accepts such a character and throws it into some situation, apprehends it in some delicate pause of life in which for a moment it becomes ideal. Take an instance from *Dramatis Personæ*. In the poem entitled 'Le Byron de nos Jours' we have a single moment of passion thrown into relief in this exquisite way. Those two jaded Parisians are not intrinsically interesting; they only begin to interest us when thrown into a choice situation. But to discriminate that moment, to make it appreciable by us, that we may 'find it', what a cobweb of allusions, what double and treble reflections of the mind upon itself, what an artificial light is constructed and broken over the chosen situation—on how fine a needle's point that little world of passion is balanced! Yet, in spite of this intricacy, the poem has the clear ring of a central motive; we receive from it the impression of one imaginative tone, of a single creative act.

To produce such effects at all requires the resources of painting, with its power of indirect expression, of subordinate but significant detail, its atmosphere, its foregrounds and backgrounds. Mr Hunt's 'Claudio and Isabella' is an instance. To produce them in a pre-eminent degree requires all the resources of poetry, language in its most purged form, its remote associations and suggestions, its double and treble lights. These appliances sculpture cannot command. In it, therefore, not the special situation, but the type, the general character of the subject to be delineated, is all-important. In poetry and painting, the situation predominates over the character; in sculpture, the character over the situation. Excluded by the limitations of its material from the development of exquisite situations, it has to choose from a select number of types intrinsically interesting—that is, independently of any special situation into which they may be thrown. Sculpture finds the secret of its power in presenting these types in their broad, central, incisive lines. This it effects not by accumulation of detail, but by abstracting from it. All that is accidental, that distracts the simple effect of the supreme types of humanity, all traces in them of the commonness of the world, it gradually purges away.

Works of art produced under this law, and only these, are really characterized by Hellenic generality or breadth. In every direction it is a law of limitation; it keeps passion always below that degree of intensity at which it is necessarily transitory, never winding up the features to one note of anger, or desire, or surprise. In the allegorical designs of the middle ages, we find isolated qualities portrayed as by so many masks; its religious art has familiarized us with faces fixed obdurately into blank types of religious sentiment; and men and women, in the hurry of life, often wear the sharp impress of one absorbing motive, from which it is said death sets their features free. All such instances may be ranged under the 'grotesque'; and the Hellenic ideal has nothing in common with the 'grotesque'. It lets passion play lightly over the surface of the individual form, which loses by it nothing of its central impassivity, its depth and repose. . . .

. . . This key to the understanding of the Greek spirit, Winckelmann possessed in his own nature—itself like a relic of classical antiquity laid open by accident to our alien modern atmosphere. To the criticism of that consummate Greek modelling he brought not only his culture, but his temperament. We have seen how definite was the leading motive of his culture; how, like some central root-fibre, it maintained the well-rounded unity of his life through a thousand distractions. Interests not his, nor meant for him—political, moral, religious—never disturbed him. In morals, as in criticism, he followed the clue of an unerring instinct. Penetrating into the antique world by his passion, his temperament, he enunciates no formal principles, always hard and one-sided; it remained for Hegel to formulate what in Winckelmann is everywhere individualized and concrete. Minute and anxious as his culture was, he never became one-sidedly self-analytical. Occupied ever with himself, perfecting himself and cultivating his genius, he was not content, as so often happens with such natures, that the atmosphere between him and other minds should be thick and clouded; he was ever jealously refining his meaning into a form, express, clear, objective. This temperament he nurtured and invigorated by friendships which kept him ever in direct contact with the spirit of youth. The beauty of the Greek statues was a sexless beauty; the statues of the gods had the least traces of sex.

Here, there is a moral sexlessness, a kind of impotence, an ineffectual wholeness of nature, yet with a divine beauty and significance of its own.

One result of this temperament is a serenity, a *Heiterkeit*, which characterizes Winckelmann's handling of the sensuous side of Greek art. This serenity is, perhaps, at bottom a negative quality; it is the absence of any sense of want, or corruption, or shame. With the sensuous of Greek art he deals in the pagan manner; and what is implied in that? It is sometimes said that art is a means of escape from 'the tyranny of the senses'. It may be so for the spectator; he may find that the spectacle of supreme works of art takes from the life of the senses something of its turbid fever. But this is possible for the spectator only because the artist in producing those works has gradually sunk his intellectual and spiritual ideas in sensuous form. He may live, as Keats lived, a pure life; but his soul, like that of Plato's false astronomer, becomes more and more immersed in sense, until nothing else has any interest for him. How could such an one ever again endure the greyness of the ideal or spiritual world? The spiritualist is satisfied in seeing the sensuous elements escape from his conceptions; his interest grows, as the dyed garment bleaches in the keener air. But the artist steeps his thought again and again into the fire of colour. To the Greek this immersion in the sensuous was indifferent. Greek sensuousness, therefore, does not fever the blood; it is shameless and childlike. But Christianity, with its uncompromising idealism, discrediting the slightest touch of sense, has lighted up for the artistic life, with its inevitable sensuousness, a background of flame. 'I did but taste a little honey with the end of the rod that was in mine hand, and lo, I must die.' It is hard to pursue that life without something of conscious disavowal of a spiritual world; and this imparts to genuine artistic interests a kind of intoxication. From this intoxication Winckelmann is free; he fingers those pagan marbles with unsinged hands, with no sense of shame or loss. That is to deal with the sensuous side of art in the pagan manner.

The longer we contemplate that Hellenic ideal in which man is at unity with himself, with his physical nature, with the outward world, the more we may be inclined to regret that he should ever have passed beyond it, to contend for a perfection that makes the blood turbid, and frets the flesh, and discredits the actual world about us. But if he was to be saved from the *ennui* which ever attaches itself to realization, even the realization of perfection, it was necessary that a conflict should come, that some sharper note should grieve the perfect harmony, in order that the spirit, chafed by it, might beat out at last a broader and profounder music. In Greek tragedy this conflict

has begun; man finds himself face to face with rival claims. Greek
tragedy shows how such a conflict may be treated with serenity,
how the evolution of it may be a spectacle of the dignity, not
of the impotence, of the human spirit.* But it is not only in tragedy
that the Greek spirit showed itself capable of thus winning joy out of
matter in itself full of discouragements. Theocritus too, often strikes
a note of romantic sadness. But what a blithe and steady poise
above these discouragements in a clear and sunny stratum of the air!

Into this stage of Greek achievement Winckelmann did not enter.
Supreme as he is where his true interest lay, his insight into the
typical unity and repose of the sculpturesque seems to have involved
limitation in another direction. His conception of art excludes that
bolder type of it which deals confidently and serenely with life,
conflict, evil. Living in a world of exquisite but abstract and colourless form, he could hardly have conceived of the subtle and penetrative, but somewhat grotesque art of the modern world. What
would he have thought of Gilliatt, or of the bleeding mouth of
Fantine in that first part of *Les Misérables*, penetrated as it is with a
sense of beauty as lively and transparent as that of a Greek? He failed
even to see, what Hegel has so cunningly detected, a sort of preparation for the romantic within the limits of the Greek ideal itself. Greek
art has not merely its mournful mysteries of Adonis, of Hyacinthus,
of Ceres, but it is conscious also of the fall of earlier divine dynasties.
Hyperion gives way to Apollo, Oceanus to Poseidon. Around the feet
of that tranquil Olympian family still crowd the weary shadows of an
earlier, more formless, divine world. Even their still minds are
troubled with thoughts of a limit to duration, of inevitable decay, of
dispossession. Again, the supreme and colourless abstraction of those
divine forms, which is the secret of their repose, is also a premonition
of the fleshless, consumptive refinements of the pale mediæval artists.
That high indifference to the outward, that impassivity, has already a
touch of the corpse in it; we see already Angelico and the 'Master of
the Passion' in the artistic future. The crushing of the sensuous, the
shutting of the door upon it, the flesh-outstripping interest, is already
traceable. Those abstracted gods, 'ready to melt out their essence
fine into the winds', who can fold up their flesh as a garment, and
remain themselves, seem already to feel that bleak air in which,
like Helen of Troy herself, they wander as the spectres of the Middle
Age.†

In this way there is imported into Hellenism something not plastic,
not sculpturesque; something 'warm, tremulous, devout, psalterian'.

* Hegel: Æsth., Th. 2, Absch. 2, Kap. 3. Die Auflösung der klassischen Kunstform.
† Hegel: Æsth., Th. 2, Absch. 3, Kap. 2.

So some of the most romantic motives of modern poetry have been borrowed from the Greek. M. Saint-Beuve says of Maurice de Guérin's 'Centaure', now so well known to English readers through Mr Arnold's essay,[3] that under the form of the Centaur Maurice *a fait son René*. He means that in it Maurice has found a vehicle for all that romantic longing which the modern temper has inherited from mediæval asceticism, and of which the *René* of Chateaubriand is the most distinguished French exponent. What is observable is that Maurice has found that vehicle in the circle of Greek mythology. This romantic element was to increase. It did not cause the decay of Hellenic art; but it shows how delicate, how rare were the conditions under which the Hellenic ideal existed, to indicate the direction which art would take in passing beyond it. In Roman hands, in the early days of Christianity, it was already falling to pieces through the loose eclecticism which characterized the age, not only in religion and philosophy, but also in literature and art. It was the age of imitators, mechanically putting together the limbs, but unable to unite them by the breath of life. Did Christianity quicken that decline? The worship of sorrow, the crucifixion of the senses, the expectation of the end of the world, are not in themselves principles of artistic rejuvenescence. Christianity in the first instance did quicken that decay. That in it which welcomed art was what was pagan in it, a fetichistic veneration for particular spots and material objects. Such materialism is capable of a thin artistic varnish, but has no natural connexion with art of a higher kind. So from the first we see Christianity taking up a few fragments of art, but not the best that the age afforded, careless of their merits; thus aiding the decline of art by consecrating it in its poorest forms.

Gradually as the world came into the church, as Christianity compromised its earlier severities, the native artistic interest reasserted its claims. But Christian art was still dependent on pagan examples, building the shafts of pagan temples into its churches, perpetuating the form of the basilica, in later times working the disused amphitheatres as quarries. The sensuous expression of conceptions which unreservedly discredit the world of sense, was the delicate problem which Christian art had before it. If we think of mediæval painting as it ranges from the early German schools, still with the air of a charnel-house about them, to the clear loveliness of Perugino, we shall see that the problem was met. Even in the worship of sorrow the native blitheness of art asserted itself; the religious spirit, as Hegel says, 'smiled through its tears'. So perfectly did the young Raphael infuse that *Heiterkeit*, that pagan blitheness, into religious works, that his picture of Saint Agatha at Bologna became to Goethe a step in the evolution of *Iphigénie*.* But in proportion as this power of smiling was refound, there came also an aspiration towards that lost antique art, some relics of which Christian art had buried in itself, ready to work wonders when their day came.

The history of art has suffered as much as any history by trenchant, absolute divisions. Pagan and Christian art are sometimes harshly opposed, and the Renaissance is represented as a fashion which set in at a definite period. That is the superficial view; the deeper is that which preserves the identity of European culture. The two are really continuous: and there is a sense in which it may be said that the Renaissance was an uninterrupted effort of the Middle Ages, that it was ever taking place. When the actual relics of the antique were restored to the world, it was to Christian eyes as if an ancient plague-pit had been opened: all the world took the contagion of the life of nature and the senses. Christian art allying itself with that restored antiquity which it had ever emulated, soon ceased to exist. For a time art dealt with Christian subjects as its patrons required; but its true freedom was in the life of the senses and the blood—blood no longer dropping from the hands in sacrifice, as with Angelico, but, as with Titian, burning in the face for desire and love. And now it was seen that the mediæval spirit, too, had done something for the destiny of the antique. By hastening the decline of art, by withdrawing interest from it, and yet keeping the thread of its traditions, it had suffered the human mind to repose, that it might awake when day came with eyes refreshed to those antique forms.

But even after the advance of the sixteenth century the Renaissance still remained in part an unfulfilled intellectual aspiration. An artificial classicism, as far as possible from the naturalism of the antique, was ready to set in if ever the Renaissance was accepted as an accomplished fact; and this was what happened. The long pilgrimage came to an end with many congratulations; only the shrine was not the genuine one. A classicism arose, based on no critical knowledge of the products of the classical spirit, unable to estimate the conditions either of its own or the classical age, regarding the adoption of the classical spirit as something facile. And yet the first condition of an historical revival is an appreciation of the differences between one age and another. The service of Winckelmann to modern culture lay in the appeal he made from the substituted text to the original. He produces the actual relics of the antique against the false tradition of the era of Louis XIV. A style or manner in art or literature can only be explained or reproduced through those special conditions

* Italiänische Reise. Bologna, 19 Oct. 1786.

of society and culture out of which it arose, and with which it forms one group of phenomena. A false classicism, in the unhistorical spirit of the age, had tried to isolate the classical manner from the group of phenomena of which it was a part; it supposed that there was some shorter way of reaching and commanding this manner than a knowledge of the vital laws of the classical mind and culture. In opposition to that classicism become a platitude, Winckelmann says, the Hellenic manner is the blossom of the Hellenic spirit and culture, that spirit and culture depend on certain conditions, and those conditions are peculiar to a certain age. Reproduce those conditions, attain the actual root, and blossoms may again be produced of a triumphant colour. The clearest note of this new criticism was the rehabilitation of Homer. Werther's preoccupation with Homer is part of the originality of his character.

The aim of a right criticism is to place Winckelmann in an intellectual perspective, of which Goethe is the foreground. For, after all, he is infinitely less than Goethe; it is chiefly because at certain points he comes in contact with Goethe that criticism entertains consideration of him. His relation to modern culture is a peculiar one. He is not of the modern world; nor is he of the eighteenth century, although so much of his outer life is characteristic of it. But that note of revolt against the eighteenth century, which we detect in Goethe, was struck by Winckelmann. Goethe illustrates that union of the Romantic, its adventure, its variety, its deep subjectivity, with Hellenism, its transparency, its rationality, its desire of beauty—that marriage of Faust and Helena, of which the art of the nineteenth century is the child, the beautiful lad Euphorion, as Goethe conceives him, on the crags in the 'splendour of battle', 'in harness as for victory', his brows bound with light.* Goethe illustrates, too, the preponderance in this marriage of the Hellenic element; and that element, in its true essence, was made known to him by Winckelmann.

Breadth, centrality, with blitheness and repose, are the marks of Hellenic culture. Is that culture a lost art? The local, accidental colouring of its own age has passed from it; the greatness that is dead looks greater when every link with what is slight and vulgar has been severed; we can only see it at all in the reflected, refined light which a high education creates for us. Can we bring down that ideal into the gaudy, perplexed light of modern life?

Certainly, for us of the modern world, with its conflicting claims, its entangled interests, distracted by so many sorrows, so many preoccupations, so bewildering an experience, the problem of unity with

* Faust, Th. 2, Act 3.

ourselves in blitheness and repose, is far harder than it was for the
Greek within the simple terms of antique life. Yet, not less than ever,
the intellect demands completeness, centrality. It is this which
Winckelmann prints on the imagination of Goethe, at the beginning
of his culture in its original and simplest form, as in a fragment of
Greek art itself stranded on that littered, indeterminate shore of
Germany in the eighteenth century. In Winckelmann this type comes
to him, not as in a book or a theory, but importunately in a passionate
life and personality. For Goethe, possessing all modern interests,
ready to be lost in the perplexed currents of modern thought, he
defines in clearest outline the problem of culture, balance, unity with
oneself, consummate Greek modelling.

It could no longer be solved, as in Phryne ascending naked out of
the water, by perfection of bodily form, or any joyful union with the
world without; the shadows had grown too long, the light too solemn
for that. It could hardly be solved as in Pericles or Phidias, by the
direct exercise of any single talent; amid the manifold claims of
modern culture that could only have ended in a thin, one-sided
growth. Goethe's Hellenism was of another order, the *Allgemeinheit*
and *Heiterkeit*, the completeness and serenity of a watchful exigent
intellectualism. *Im Ganzen, Guten, Wahren, resolut zu leben*, is Goethe's
description of his own higher life; and what is meant by life in the
whole, *im Ganzen*? It means the life of one for whom, over and over
again, what was once precious has become indifferent. Every one who
aims at the life of culture is met by many forms of it, arising out of the
intense, laborious, one-sided development of some special talent.
They are the brightest enthusiasms the world has to show. They do
not care to weigh the claims which this or that alien form of culture
makes upon them. But the pure instinct of self-culture cares not so
much to reap all that these forms of culture can give, as to find in
them its own strength. The demand of the intellect is to feel itself
alive. It must see into the laws, the operation, the intellectual reward
of every divided form of culture; but only that it may measure the
relation between itself and them. It struggles with those forms till its
secret is won from each, and then lets each fall back into its place in
the supreme, artistic view of life. With a kind of passionate coldness
such natures rejoice to be away from and past their former selves.
Above all, they are jealous of that *abandon* to one special gift which
really limits their capabilities. It would have been easy for Goethe,
with the gift of a sensuous nature, to let it overgrow him. But the
utmost a sensuous gift can produce are the poems of Keats, or the
paintings of Giorgione; and often in some stray line of Shakespeare,
some fleeting tone of Raphael, the whole power of Keats or Giorgione

strikes on one from its due place in a complete composite nature. It is easy with the other worldly gifts to be a *schöne Seele*; but to the large vision of Goethe that seemed to be a phase of life that a man might feel all round and leave behind him. Again, it is easy to indulge the common-place metaphysical instinct. But a taste for metaphysics may be one of those things which we must renounce if we mean to mould our lives to artistic perfection. Philosophy serves culture not by the fancied gift of absolute or transcendental knowledge, but by suggesting questions which help one to detect the passion and strangeness and dramatic contrasts of life.

But Goethe's culture did not remain 'behind the veil'; it ever abutted on the practical functions of art, on actual production. For him the problem came to be, can the *Allgemeinheit*, the *Heiterkeit* of the antique be communicated to artistic productions which contain the fulness of the experience of the modern world? We have seen that the development of the various forms of art has corresponded to the development of the thoughts of man concerning himself, to the growing relation of the mind to itself.[4] Sculpture corresponds to the unperplexed, emphatic outlines of Hellenic humanism; painting to the mystic depth and intricacy of the Middle Age; music and poetry have their fortune in the modern world. Let us understand by poetry all literary production which attains the power of giving joy by its form as distinct from its matter. Only in this varied literary form can art command that width, variety, delicacy of resources, which will enable it to deal with the conditions of modern life. What modern art has to do in the service of culture is so to rearrange the details of modern life, so to reflect it, that it may satisfy the spirit. And what does the spirit need in the face of modern life? The sense of freedom. That naïve, rough sense of freedom, which supposes man's will to be limited if at all only by a will stronger than his, he can never have again. The attempt to represent it in art would have so little verisimilitude that it would be flat and uninteresting. The chief factor in the thoughts of the modern mind concerning itself is the intricacy, the universality of natural law even in the moral order. For us necessity is not as of old an image without us, with whom we can do warfare; it is a magic web woven through and through us, like that magnetic system of which modern science speaks, penetrating us with a network subtler than our subtlest nerves, yet bearing in it the central forces of the world. Can art represent men and women in these bewildering toils so as to give the spirit at least an equivalent for the sense of freedom? Goethe's *Wahlverwandtschaften* is a high instance of modern art dealing thus with modern life: it regards that life as the modern mind must regard it, but reflects upon it blitheness and repose.

Natural laws we shall never modify, embarrass us as they may; but there is still something in the nobler or less noble attitude with which we watch their fatal combinations. In *Wahlverwandtschaften* this entanglement, this network of law, becomes a tragic situation, in which a group of noble men and women work out a supreme *dénoue-ment*. Who, if he foresaw all, would fret against circumstances which endow one at the end with so high an experience?

CONCLUSION[1] TO *THE RENAISSANCE*

Λέγει που Ἡράκλειτος ὅτι πάντα χωρεῖ καὶ οὐδὲν μένει.[2]

To regard all things and principles of things as inconstant modes or fashions has more and more become the tendency of modern thought. Let us begin with that which is without—our physical life. Fix upon it in one of its more exquisite intervals, the moment, for instance, of delicious recoil from the flood of water in summer heat. What is the whole physical life in that moment but a combination of natural elements to which science gives their names? But these elements, phosphorus and lime and delicate fibres, are present not in the human body alone: we detect them in places most remote from it. Our physical life is a perpetual motion of them—the passage of the blood, the wasting and repairing of the lenses of the eye, the modification of the tissues of the brain by every ray of light and sound—processes which science reduces to simpler and more elementary forces. Like the elements of which we are composed, the action of these forces extends beyond us; it rusts iron and ripens corn. Far out on every side of us these elements are broadcast, driven by many forces;[3] and birth and gesture and death and the springing of violets from the grave are but a few out of ten thousand resulting combinations. That clear perpetual outline of face and limb is but an image of ours under which we group them—a design in a web, the actual threads of which pass out beyond it. This at least of flame-like our life has, that it is but the concurrence, renewed from moment to moment, of forces parting sooner or later on their ways.

Or if we begin with the inward world of thought and feeling, the whirlpool is still more rapid, the flame more eager and devouring. There it is no longer the gradual darkening of the eye and fading of colour from the wall,—the movement of the shore side, where the water flows down indeed, though in apparent rest,—but the race of the midstream, a drift of momentary acts of sight and passion and thought. At first sight experience seems to bury us under a flood of external objects, pressing upon us with a sharp importunate reality, calling us out of ourselves in a thousand forms of action. But when

39

reflection begins to act upon those objects they are dissipated under its influence; the cohesive force is suspended like a trick of magic; each object is loosed into a group of impressions,—colour, odour, texture,—in the mind of the observer. And if we continue to dwell on this world, not of objects in the solidity with which language invests them, but of impressions unstable, flickering, inconsistent, which burn and are extinguished with our consciousness of them, it contracts still further; the whole scope of observation is dwarfed to the narrow chamber of the individual mind. Experience, already reduced to a swarm of impressions, is ringed round for each one of us by that thick wall of personality through which no real voice has ever pierced on its way to us, or from us to that which we can only conjecture to be without. Every one of those impressions is the impression of the individual in his isolation, each mind keeping as a solitary prisoner its own dream of a world.

Analysis goes a step further still, and tells us that those impressions of the individual to which, for each one of us, experience dwindles down, are in perpetual flight; that each of them is limited by time, and that as time is infinitely divisible, each of them is infinitely divisible also; all that is actual in it being a single moment, gone while we try to apprehend it, of which it may ever be more truly said that it has ceased to be than that it is. To such a tremulous wisp constantly reforming itself on the stream, to a single sharp impression, with a sense in it, a relic more or less fleeting, of such moments gone by, what is *real* in our life fines itself down. It is with the movement, the passage and dissolution of impressions, images, sensations, that analysis leaves off,—that continual vanishing away, that strange perpetual weaving and unweaving of ourselves.

Philosophiren, says Novalis, *ist dephlegmatisiren, vivificiren.* The service of philosophy, and of religion [4] and culture as well, to the human spirit, is to startle it into a sharp and eager observation. Every moment some form grows perfect in hand or face; some tone on the hills or sea is choicer than the rest; some mood of passion or insight or intellectual excitement is irresistibly real and attractive for us,—for that moment only. Not the fruit of experience, but experience itself is the end. A counted number of pulses only is given to us of a variegated, dramatic life. How may we see in them all that is to be seen in them by the finest senses? How can we pass most swiftly from point to point, and be present always at the focus where the greatest number of vital forces unite in their purest energy?

To burn always with this hard gem-like flame, to maintain this ecstasy, is success in life. Failure is to form habits; [5] for habit is relative to a stereotyped world; meantime it is only the roughness of the eye that makes any two persons, things, situations, seem alike. While all melts under our feet, we may well catch at any exquisite passion, or any contribution to knowledge that seems, by a lifted horizon, to set the spirit free for a moment, or any stirring of the senses, strange dyes, strange flowers, and curious odours, or work of the artist's hands, or the face of one's friend. Not to discriminate every moment some passionate attitude in those about us, and in the brilliance of their gifts some tragic dividing of forces on their ways is, on this short day of frost and sun, to sleep before evening. With this sense of the splendour of our experience and of its awful brevity, gathering all we are into one desperate effort to see and touch, we shall hardly have time to make theories about the things we see and touch. What we have to do is to be for ever curiously testing new opinions and courting new impressions, never acquiescing in a facile orthodoxy of Comte or of Hegel, or of our own. Theories,[6] religious or philosophical ideas, as points of view, instruments of criticism, may help us to gather up what might otherwise pass unregarded by us. *La philosophie, c'est la microscope de la pensée.* The theory, or idea, or system, which requires of us the sacrifice of any part of this experience, in consideration of some interest into which we cannot enter, or some abstract morality we have not identified with ourselves, or what is only conventional, has no real claim upon us.

One of the most beautiful places in the writings of Rousseau is that in the sixth book of the 'Confessions', where he describes the awakening in him of the literary sense. An undefinable taint of death had always clung about him, and now in early manhood he believed himself stricken by mortal disease. He asked himself how he might make as much as possible of the interval that remained; and he was not biassed by anything in his previous life when he decided that it must be by intellectual excitement, which he found in the clear, fresh writings of Voltaire. Well, we are all *condamnés*, as Victor Hugo says: *les hommes sont tous condamnés a morte avec des sursis indéfinis:* we have an interval, and then our place knows us no more. Some spend this interval in listlessness, some in high passions, the wisest in art and song. For our one chance is in expanding that interval, in getting as many pulsations as possible into the given time. High passions give one this quickened sense of life, ecstasy and sorrow of love,[7] political or religious enthusiasm, or the 'enthusiasm of humanity'. Only, be sure it is passion, that it does yield you this fruit of a quickened, multiplied consciousness. Of this wisdom, the poetic passion, the desire of beauty, the love of art for art's sake has most; for art comes to you professing frankly to give nothing but the highest quality to your moments as they pass, and simply for those moments' sake.[8]

The Dialectic of Art

THE SCHOOL OF GIORGIONE[1]

It is the mistake of much popular criticism to regard poetry, music, and painting—all the various products of art—as but translations into different languages of one and the same fixed quantity of imaginative thought, supplemented by certain technical qualities of colour, in painting; of sound, in music; of rhythmical words, in poetry. In this way, the sensuous element in art, and with it almost everything in art that is essentially artistic, is made a matter of indifference; and a clear apprehension of the opposite principle—that the sensuous material of each art brings with it a special phase or quality of beauty, untranslatable into the forms of any other, an order of impressions distinct in kind—is the beginning of all true æsthetic criticism. For, as art addresses not pure sense, still less the pure intellect, but the 'imaginative reason' through the senses, there are differences of kind in æsthetic beauty, corresponding to the differences in kind of the gifts of sense themselves. Each art, therefore, having its own peculiar and untranslatable sensuous charm, has its own special mode of reaching the imagination, its own special responsibilities to its material. One of the functions of æsthetic criticism is to define these limitations; to estimate the degree in which a given work of art fulfils its responsibilities to its special material; to note in a picture that true pictorial charm, which is neither a mere poetical thought or sentiment, on the one hand, nor a mere result of communicable technical skill in colour or design, on the other; to define in a poem that true poetical quality, which is neither descriptive nor meditative merely, but comes of an inventive handling of rhythmical language, the element of song in the singing; to note in music the musical charm, that essential music, which presents no words, no matter of sentiment or thought, separable from the special form in which it is conveyed to us.

To such a philosophy of the variations of the beautiful, Lessing's analysis of the spheres of sculpture and poetry, in the *Laocoon*,[2] was an important contribution. But a true appreciation of these things is possible only in the light of a whole system of such art-casuistries.

43

Now painting is the art in the criticism of which this truth most needs enforcing, for it is in popular judgments on pictures that the false generalisation of all art into forms of poetry is most prevalent. To suppose that all is mere technical acquirement in delineation or touch, working through and addressing itself to the intelligence, on the one side, or a merely poetical, or what may be called literary interest, addressed also to the pure intelligence, on the other:—this is the way of most spectators, and of many critics, who have never caught sight all the time of that true pictorial quality which lies between, unique pledge, as it is, of the possession of the pictorial gift, that inventive or creative handling of pure line and colour, which, as almost always in Dutch painting, as often also in the works of Titian or Veronese, is quite independent of anything definitely poetical in the subject it accompanies. It is the *drawing*—the design projected from that peculiar pictorial temperament or constitution, in which, while it may possibly be ignorant of true anatomical proportions, all things whatever, all poetry, all ideas however abstract or obscure, float up as visible scene or image: it is the *colouring*—that weaving of light, as of just perceptible gold threads, through the dress, the flesh, the atmosphere, in Titian's *Lace-girl*, that staining of the whole fabric of the thing with a new, delightful physical quality. This *drawing*, then—the arabesque traced in the air by Tintoret's flying figures, by Titian's forest branches; this colouring—the magic conditions of light and hue in the atmosphere of Titian's *Lace-girl*, or Rubens's *Descent from the Cross:*—these essential pictorial qualities must first of all delight the sense, delight it as directly and sensuously as a fragment of Venetian glass; and through this delight alone become the vehicle of whatever poetry or science may lie beyond them in the intention of the composer. In its primary aspect, a great picture has no more definite message for us than an accidental play of sunlight and shadow for a few moments on the wall or floor: is itself, in truth, a space of such fallen light, caught as the colours are in an Eastern carpet, but refined upon, and dealt with more subtly and exquisitely than by nature itself. And this primary and essential condition fulfilled, we may trace the coming of poetry into painting, by fine gradations upwards; from Japanese fan-painting, for instance, where we get, first, only abstract colour; then, just a little interfused sense of the poetry of flowers; then, sometimes, perfect flower-painting; and so, onwards, until in Titian we have, as his poetry in the *Ariadne*, so actually a touch of true childlike humour in the diminutive, quaint figure with its silk gown, which ascends the temple stairs, in his picture of the *Presentation of the Virgin*, at Venice.

But although each art has thus its own specific order of impressions,

and an untranslatable charm, while a just apprehension of the
ultimate differences of the arts is the beginning of æsthetic criticism;
yet it is noticeable that, in its special mode of handling its given
material, each art may be observed to pass into the condition of some
other art, by what German critics term an *Anders-streben*—a partial
alienation from its own limitations, through which the arts are able,
not indeed to supply the place of each other, but reciprocally to lend
each other new forces.[3]

Thus some of the most delightful music seems to be always approaching to figure, to pictorial definition. Architecture, again,
though it has its own laws—laws esoteric enough, as the true architect
knows only too well—yet sometimes aims at fulfilling the conditions
of a picture, as in the *Arena* chapel; or of sculpture, as in the flawless
unity of Giotto's tower at Florence; and often finds a true poetry, as
in those strangely twisted staircases of the *châteaux* of the country of
the Loire, as if it were intended that among their odd turnings the
actors in a theatrical mode of life might pass each other unseen; there
being a poetry also of memory and of the mere effect of time, by
which architecture often profits greatly. Thus, again, sculpture aspires
out of the hard limitation of pure form towards colour, or its
equivalent; poetry also, in many ways, finding guidance from the
other arts, the analogy between a Greek tragedy and a work of Greek
sculpture, between a sonnet and a relief, of French poetry generally
with the art of engraving, being more than mere figures of speech;
and all the arts in common aspiring towards the principle of music;
music being the typical, or ideally consummate art, the object of the
great *Anders-streben* of all art, of all that is artistic, or partakes of
artistic qualities.

All art constantly aspires towards the condition of music.[4] For while in all
other kinds of art it is possible to distinguish the matter from the form,
and the understanding can always make this distinction, yet it is the
constant effort of art to obliterate it. That the mere matter of a poem,
for instance, its subject, namely, its given incidents or situation—that
the mere matter of a picture, the actual circumstances of an event, the
actual topography of a landscape—should be nothing without the
form, the spirit, of the handling, that this form, this mode of handling,
should become an end in itself, should penetrate every part of the
matter: this is what all art constantly strives after, and achieves in
different degrees.

This abstract language becomes clear enough, if we think of actual
examples. In an actual landscape we see a long white road, lost
suddenly on the hill-verge. This is the matter of one of the etchings of
M. Alphonse Legros: only, in this etching, it is informed by an

indwelling solemnity of expression, seen upon it or half-seen, within the limits of an exceptional moment, or caught from his own mood perhaps, but which he maintains as the very essence of the thing throughout his work. Sometimes a momentary hint of stormy light may invest a homely or too familiar scene with a character which might well have been drawn from the deep places of the imagination. Then we might say that this particular effect of light, this sudden inweaving of gold thread through the texture of the haystack, and the poplars, and the grass, gives the scene artistic qualities, that it is like a picture. And such tricks of circumstance are commonest in landscape which has little salient character of its own; because, in such scenery, all the material details are so easily absorbed by that informing expression of passing light, and elevated, throughout their whole extent, to a new and delightful effect by it. And hence the superiority, for most conditions of the picturesque, of a riverside in France to a Swiss valley, because, on the French river-side, mere topography, the simple material, counts for so little, and, all being very pure, untouched, and tranquil in itself, mere light and shade have such easy work in modulating it to one dominant tone. The Venetian landscape, on the other hand, has in its material conditions much which is hard, or harshly definite; but the masters of the Venetian school have shown themselves little burdened by them. Of its Alpine background they retain certain abstracted elements only, of cool colour and tranquillising line; and they use its actual details, the brown windy turrets, the straw-coloured fields, the forest arabesques, but as the notes of a music which duly accompanies the presence of their men and women, presenting us with the spirit or essence only of a certain sort of landsbape—a country of the pure reason or half-imaginative memory.

Poetry, again, works with words addressed in the first instance to the pure intelligence; and it deals, most often, with a definite subject or situation. Sometimes it may find a noble and quite legitimate function in the conveyance of moral or political aspiration, as often in the poetry of Victor Hugo. In such instances it is easy enough for the understanding to distinguish between the matter and the form, however much the matter, the subject, the element which is addressed to the mere intelligence, has been penetrated by the informing, artistic spirit. But the ideal types of poetry are those in which this distinction is reduced to its *minimum*; so that lyrical poetry, precisely because in it we are least able to detach the matter from the form, without a deduction of something from that matter itself, is, at least artistically, the highest and most complete form of poetry. And the very perfection of such poetry often appears to depend, in part, on a certain suppression or vagueness of mere subject, so that the meaning reaches us through ways not distinctly traceable by the understanding, as in some of the most imaginative compositions of William Blake, and often in Shakespeare's songs, as pre-eminently in that song of Mariana's page in *Measure for Measure*, in which the kindling force and poetry of the whole play seems to pass for a moment into an actual strain of music.

And this principle holds good of all things that partake in any degree of artistic qualities, of the furniture of our houses, and of dress, for instance, of life itself, of gesture and speech, and the details of daily intercourse; these also, for the wise, being susceptible of a suavity and charm, caught from the way in which they are done, which gives them a worth in themselves. Herein, again, lies what is valuable and justly attractive, in what is called the fashion of a time, which elevates the trivialities of speech, and manner, and dress, into 'ends in themselves', and gives them a mysterious grace and attractiveness in the doing of them.

Art, then, is thus always striving to be independent of the mere intelligence, to become a matter of pure perception, to get rid of its responsibilities to its subject or material; the ideal examples of poetry and painting being those in which the constituent elements of the composition are so welded together, that the material or subject no longer strikes the intellect only; nor the form, the eye or the ear only; but form and matter, in their union or identity, present one single effect to the 'imaginative reason', that complex faculty for which every thought and feeling is twin-born with its sensible analogue or symbol.

It is the art of music which most completely realises this artistic ideal, this perfect identification of matter and form. In its consummate moments, the end is not distinct from the means, the form from the matter, the subject from the expression; they inhere in and completely saturate each other; and to it, therefore, to the condition of its perfect moments, all the arts may be supposed constantly to tend and aspire. In music, then, rather than in poetry, is to be found the true type or measure of perfected art. Therefore, although each art has its incommunicable element, its untranslatable order of impressions, its unique mode of reaching the 'imaginative reason', yet the arts may be represented as continually struggling after the law or principle of music, to a condition which music alone completely realises; and one of the chief functions of æsthetic criticism, dealing with the products of art, new or old, is to estimate the degree in which each of those products approaches, in this sense, to musical law.

POSTSCRIPT[1] TO *APPRECIATIONS*

αἰνεῖ δὲ παλαιὸν μὲν οἶνον, ἄνθεα δ' ὕμνων νεωτέρων [2]

The words, *classical* and *romantic*, although, like many other critical expressions, sometimes abused by those who have understood them too vaguely or too absolutely, yet define two real tendencies in the history of art and literature. Used in an exaggerated sense, to express a greater opposition between those tendencies than really exists, they have at times tended to divide people of taste into opposite camps. But in that *House Beautiful*, which the creative minds of all generations —the artists and those who have treated life in the spirit of art—are always building together, for the refreshment of the human spirit, these oppositions cease; and the *Interpreter* of the *House Beautiful*,[3] the true æsthetic critic, uses these divisions, only so far as they enable him to enter into the pecularities of the objects with which he has to do. The term *classical*, fixed, as it is, to a well-defined literature, and a well-defined group in art, is clear, indeed; but then it has often been used in a hard, and merely scholastic sense, by the praisers of what is old and accustomed, at the expense of what is new, by critics who would never have discovered for themselves the charm of any work, whether new or old, who value what is old, in art or literature, for its accessories, and chiefly for the conventional authority that has gathered about it—people who would never really have been made glad by any Venus fresh-risen from the sea, and who praise the Venus of old Greece and Rome, only because they fancy her grown now into something staid and tame.

And as the term, *classical*, has been used in a too absolute, and therefore in a misleading sense, so the term, *romantic*, has been used much too vaguely, in various accidental senses. The sense in which Scott is called a romantic writer is chiefly this; that, in opposition to the literary tradition of the last century, he loved strange adventure, and sought it in the Middle Age. Much later, in a Yorkshire village, the spirit of romanticism bore a more really characteristic fruit in the work of a young girl, Emily Brontë, the romance of *Wuthering Heights*;

48

the figures of Hareton Earnshaw, of Catherine Linton, and of Heathcliffe—tearing open Catherine's grave, removing one side of her coffin, that he may really lie beside her in death—figures so passionate, yet woven on a background of delicately beautiful, moorland scenery, being typical examples of that spirit. In Germany, again, that spirit is shown less in Tieck, its professional representative, than in Meinhold, the author of *Sidonia the Sorceress* and the *Amber-Witch*. In Germany and France, within the last hundred years, the term has been used to describe a particular school of writers; and, consequently, when Heine criticises the *Romantic School* in Germany— that movement which culminated in Goethe's *Goetz von Berlichingen*; or when Théophile Gautier criticises the romantic movement in France, where, indeed, it bore its most characteristic fruits, and its play is hardly yet over where, by a certain audacity, or *bizarrerie* of motive, united with faultless literary execution, it still shows itself in imaginative literature, they use the word, with an exact sense of special artistic qualities, indeed; but use it, nevertheless, with a limited application to the manifestation of those qualities at a par- ticular period. But the romantic spirit is, in reality, an ever-present, an enduring principle, in the artistic temperament; and the qualities of thought and style which that, and other similar uses of the word *romantic* really indicate, are indeed but symptoms of a very continuous and widely working influence.

Though the words *classical* and *romantic*, then, have acquired an almost technical meaning, in application to certain developments of German and French taste, yet this is but one variation of an old opposition, which may be traced from the very beginning of the forma- tion of European art and literature. From the first formation of any- thing like a standard of taste in these things, the restless curiosity of their more eager lovers necessarily made itself felt, in the craving for new motives, new subjects of interest, new modifications of style. Hence, the opposition between the classicists and the romanticists— between the adherents, in the culture of beauty, of the principles of liberty, and authority, respectively—of strength, and order or what the Greeks called κοσμιότης.

Saint-Beuve, in the third volume of the *Causeries du Lundi*, has discussed the question, *What is meant by a classic?* It was a question he was well fitted to answer, having himself lived through many phases of taste, and having been in earlier life an enthusiastic member of the romantic school: he was also a great master of that sort of 'philosophy of literature', which delights in tracing traditions in it, and the way in which various phases of thought and sentiment maintain them- selves, through successive modifications, from epoch to epoch. His aim, then, is to give the word *classic* a wider and, as he says, a more generous sense than it commonly bears, to make it expressly *grandiose et flottant*; and, in doing this, he develops, in a masterly manner, those qualities of measure, purity, temperance, of which it is the especial function of classical art and literature, whatever meaning, narrower or wider, we attach to the term, to take care.

The charm, therefore, of what is classical, in art or literature, is that of the well-known tale, to which we can, nevertheless, listen over and over again, because it is told so well. To the absolute beauty of its artistic form, is added the accidental, tranquil, charm of familiarity. There are times, indeed, at which these charms fail to work on our spirits at all, because they fail to excite us. '*Romanticism*', says Stendhal, 'is the art of presenting to people the literary works which, in the actual state of their habits and beliefs, are capable of giving them the greatest possible pleasure; *classicism*, on the contrary, of presenting them with that which gave the greatest possible pleasure to their grandfathers.' But then beneath all changes of habits and beliefs, our love of that mere abstract proportion—of music—which what is classical in literature possesses, still maintains itself in the best of us, and what pleased our grandparents may at least tranquillise us. The 'classic' comes to us out of the cool and quiet of other times, as the measure of what a long experience has shown will at least never displease us. And in the classical literature of Greece and Rome, as in the classics of the last century, the essentially classical element is that quality of order in beauty, which they possess, indeed, in a preeminent degree, and which impresses some minds to the exclusion of everything else in them.

It is the addition of strangeness to beauty, that constitutes the romantic character in art; and the desire of beauty being a fixed element in every artistic organisation, it is the addition of curiosity to this desire of beauty, that constitutes the romantic temper. Curiosity and the desire of beauty, have each their place in art, as in all true criticism. When one's curiosity is deficient, when one is not eager enough for new impressions, and new pleasures, one is liable to value mere academical properties too highly, to be satisfied with worn-out or conventional types, with the insipid ornament of Racine,[3] or the prettiness of that later Greek sculpture, which passed so long for true Hellenic work; to miss those places where the handiwork of nature, or of the artist, has been most cunning; to find the most stimulating products of art a mere irritation. And when one's curiosity is in excess, when it overbalances the desire of beauty, then one is liable to value in works of art what is inartistic in them; to be satisfied with what is exaggerated in art, with productions like some of those of the romantic school in Germany; not to distinguish, jealously enough, between what is admirably done, and what is done not quite so well, in the writings, for instance, of Jean Paul. And if I had to give instances of these defects, then I should say, that Pope, in common with the age of literature to which he belonged, had too little curiosity, so that there is always a certain insipidity in the effect of his work, exquisite as it is; and, coming down to our own time, that Balzac had an excess of curiosity—curiosity not duly tempered with the desire of beauty.

But, however falsely those two tendencies may be opposed by critics, or exaggerated by artists themselves, they are tendencies really at work at all times in art, moulding it, with the balance sometimes a little on one side, sometimes a little on the other, generating, respectively, as the balance inclines on this side or that, two principles, two traditions, in art, and in literature so far as it partakes of the spirit of art. If there is a great overbalance of curiosity, then, we have the grotesque in art: if the union of strangeness and beauty, under very difficult and complex conditions, be a successful one, if the union be entire, then the resultant beauty is very exquisite, very attractive. With a passionate care for beauty, the romantic spirit refuses to have it, unless the condition of strangeness be first fulfilled. Its desire is for a beauty born of unlikely elements, by a profound alchemy, by a difficult initiation, by the charm which wrings it even out of terrible things; and a trace of distortion, of the grotesque, may perhaps linger, as an additional element of expression, about its ultimate grace. Its eager, excited spirit will have strength, the grotesque, first of all—the trees shrieking as you tear off the leaves; for Jean Valjean, the long years of convict life; for Redgauntlet, the quicksands of Solway Moss; then, incorporate with this strangeness, and intensified by restraint, as much sweetness, as much beauty, as is compatible with that. *Énergique, frais, et dispos*—these, according to Sainte-Beuve, are the characteristics of a genuine classic—*les ouvrages anciens ne sont pas classiques parce qu'ils sont vieux, mais parce qu'ils sont énergiques, frais, et dispos*. Energy, freshness, intelligent and masterly disposition:— these are characteristics of Victor Hugo when his alchemy is complete, in certain figures, like Marius and Cosette, in certain scenes, like that in the opening of *Les Travailleurs de la Mer*, where Déruchette writes the name of *Gilliatt* in the snow, on Christmas morning; but always there is a certain note of strangeness discernible there, as well.

The essential elements, then, of the romantic spirit are curiosity and the love of beauty; and it is only as an illustration of these qualities, that it seeks the Middle Age, because, in the overcharged atmosphere of the Middle Age, there are unworked sources of romantic effect, of a strange beauty, to be won, by strong imagination, out of things unlikely or remote.

Few, probably, now read Madame de Staël's *De l'Allemagne*, though it has its interest, the interest which never quite fades out of work really touched with the enthusiasm of the spiritual adventurer, the pioneer in culture. It was published in 1810, to introduce to French readers a new school of writers—the romantic school, from beyond the Rhine; and it was followed, twenty-three years later, by Heine's *Romantische Schule*, as at once a supplement and a correction. Both these books, then, connect romanticism with Germany, with the names especially of Goethe and Tieck; and, to many English readers, the idea of romanticism is still inseparably connected with Germany—that Germany which, in its quaint old towns, under the spire of Strasburg or the towers of Heidelberg, was always listening in rapt inaction to the melodious, fascinating voices of the Middle Age, and which, now that it has got Strasburg back again, has, I suppose, almost ceased to exist. But neither Germany, with its Goethe and Tieck, nor England, with its Byron and Scott, is nearly so representative of the romantic temper as France, with Murger, and Gautier, and Victor Hugo. It is in French literature that its most characteristic expression is to be found; and that, as most closely derivative, historically, from such peculiar conditions, as ever reinforce it to the utmost.

For, although temperament has much to do with the generation of the romantic spirit, and although this spirit, with its curiosity, its thirst for a curious beauty, may be always traceable in excellent art (traceable even in Sophocles) yet still, in a limited sense, it may be said to be a product of special epochs. Outbreaks of this spirit that is, come naturally with particular periods—times, when, in men's approaches towards art and poetry, curiosity may be noticed to take the lead, when men come to art and poetry, with a deep thirst for intellectual excitement, after a long *ennui*, or in reaction against the strain of outward, practical things: in the later Middle Age, for instance; so that medieval poetry, centering in Dante, is often opposed to Greek and Roman poetry, as romantic poetry to the classical. What the romanticism of Dante is, may be estimated, if we compare the lines in which Virgil describes the hazelwood, from whose broken twigs flows the blood of Polydorus, not without the expression of a real shudder at the ghastly incident, with the whole canto of the *Inferno*, into which Dante has expanded them, beautifying and softening it, meanwhile, by a sentiment of profound pity. And it is especially in that period of intellectual disturbance, immediately preceding Dante, amid which the romance languages define themselves at last, that this temper is manifested. Here, in the literature of Provence, the very name of *romanticism* is stamped with its true signification: here we have indeed a romantic world, grotesque even, in the strength of its passions, almost insane in its curious expression of them, drawing all things into its sphere, making the birds, nay! lifeless things, its voices and messengers, yet so penetrated with the desire for beauty and sweetness, that it begets a wholly new species of poetry, in which the *Renaissance* may be said to begin.[4] The last century was pre-eminently a classical age, an age in which, for art and literature, the element of a comely order was in the ascendant; which, passing away, left a hard battle to be fought between the classical and the romantic schools. Yet, it is in the heart of this century, of Goldsmith and Stothard, of Watteau and the *Siècle de Louis XIV.*—in one of its central, if not most characteristic figures, in Rousseau—that the modern or French romanticism really originates. But, what in the eighteenth century is but an exceptional phenomenon, breaking through its fair reserve and discretion only at rare intervals, is the habitual guise of the nineteenth, breaking through it perpetually, with a feverishness, an incomprehensible straining and excitement, which all experience to some degree, but yearning also, in the genuine children of the romantic school, to be *énergique, frais, et dispos*—for those qualities of energy, freshness, comely order; and often, in Murger, in Gautier, in Victor Hugo, for instance, with singular felicity attaining them.

It is in this terrible tragedy of Rousseau, in fact, that French romanticism, with much else, begins: reading his *Confessions* we seem actually to assist at the birth of this new, strong spirit in the French mind. The wildness which has shocked so many, and the fascination which has influenced almost every one, in the squalid, yet eloquent figure, we see and hear so clearly in that book, wandering under the apple-blossoms and among the vines of Neuchâtel or Vevey actually give it the quality of a very successful romantic invention. His strangeness or distortion, his profound subjectivity, his passionateness —the *cor laceratum*—Rousseau makes all men in love with these. *Je ne suis fait comme aucun de ceux que j'ai sus. Mais si je ne vaux pas mieux, au moins je suis autre.*—'I am not made like any one else I have ever known: yet, if I am not better, at least I am different.' These words, from the first page of the *Confessions*, anticipate all the Werthers, Renés, Obermanns, of the last hundred years. For Rousseau did but anticipate a trouble in the spirit of the whole world; and thirty years afterwards, what in him was a peculiarity, became part of the general consciousness. A storm was coming: Rousseau, with others, felt it in the air, and they helped to bring it down: they introduced a disturbing element into French literature, then so trim and formal, like our own literature of the age of Queen Anne.

In 1815 the storm had come and gone, but had left, in the spirit of 'young France', the *ennui* of an immense disillusion. In the last chapter of Edgar Quinet's *Révolution Française*, a work itself full of irony, of disillusion, he distinguishes two books, Senancour's *Obermann* and Chateaubriand's *Génie du Christianisme*, as characteristic of the first decade of the present century. In those two books we detect already the disease and the cure—in *Obermann* the irony, refined into a plaintive philosophy of 'indifference'—in Chateaubriand's *Génie du Christianisme*, the refuge from a tarnished actual present, a present of disillusion, into a world of strength and beauty in the Middle Age, as at an earlier period—in *René* and *Atala*—into the free play of them in savage life. It is to minds in this spiritual situation, weary of the present, but yearning for the spectacle of beauty and strength, that the works of French romanticism appeal. They set a positive value on the intense, the exceptional; and a certain distortion is sometimes noticeable in them, as in conceptions like Victor Hugo's *Quasimodo*, or *Gwynplaine*, something of a terrible grotesque, of the *macabre*, as the French themselves call it; though always combined with perfect literary execution, as in Gautier's *La Morte Amoureuse*, or the scene of the 'maimed' burial-rites of the player, dead of the frost, in his *Capitaine Fracasse*—true 'flowers of the yew'. It becomes grim humour in Victor Hugo's combat of Gilliatt with the devil-fish, or the incident, with all its ghastly comedy drawn out at length, of the great gun detached from its fastenings on shipboard, in *Quatre-Vingt-Trieze* (perhaps the most terrible of all the accidents that can happen by sea) and in the entire episode, in that book, of the *Convention*. Not less surely does it reach a genuine pathos; for the habit of noting and distinguishing one's own most intimate passages of sentiment makes one sympathetic, begetting, as it must, the power of entering, by all sorts of finer ways, into the intimate recesses of other minds; so that pity is another quality of romanticism, both Victor Hugo and Gautier being great lovers of animals, and charming writers about them, and Murger being unrivalled in the pathos of his *Scènes de la Vie de Jeunesse*. Penetrating so finely into all situations which appeal to pity, above all, into the special or exceptional phases of such feeling, the romantic humour is not afraid of the quaintness or singularity of its circumstances or expression, pity, indeed, being of the essence of humour; so that Victor Hugo does but turn his romanticism into practice, in his hunger and thirst after practical *Justice!*—a justice which shall no longer wrong children, or animals, for instance, by ignoring in a stupid, mere breadth of view, minute facts about them. Yet the romanticists are antinomian, too, sometimes, because the love of energy and beauty, of distinction in passion, tended naturally to become a little *bizarre*, plunging into the Middle Age, into the secrets of old Italian story. *Are we in the Inferno?*—we are tempted to ask, wondering at something malign in so much beauty. For over all a care for the refreshment of the human spirit by fine art manifests itself, a predominant sense of literary charm, so that, in their search for the secret of exquisite expression, the romantic school went back to the forgotten world of early French poetry, and literature itself became the most delicate of the arts—like 'goldsmith's work', says Sainte-Beuve, of Bertrand's *Gaspard de la Nuit*—and that peculiarly French gift, the gift of exquisite speech, *argute loqui*, attained in them a perfection which it had never seen before.

Stendhal, a writer whom I have already quoted, and of whom English readers might well know much more than they do, stands between the earlier and later growths of the romantic spirit. His novels are rich in romantic quality; and his other writings—partly criticism, partly personal reminiscences—are a very curious and interesting illustration of the needs out of which romanticism arose. In his book on *Racine and Shakespeare*, Stendhal argues that all good art was romantic in its day; and this is perhaps true in Stendhal's sense. That little treatise, full of 'dry light' and fertile ideas, was published in the year 1823, and its object is to defend an entire independence and liberty in the choice and treatment of subject, both in art and literature, against those who upheld the exclusive authority of precedent. In pleading the cause of romanticism, therefore, it is the novelty, both of form and of motive, in writings like the *Hernani* of Victor Hugo (which soon followed it, raising a storm of criticism) that he is chiefly concerned to justify. To be interesting and really stimulating, to keep us from yawning even, art and literature must follow the subtle movements of that nimbly-shifting *Time-Spirit*, or *Zeit-Geist*, understood by French not less than by German criticism, which is always modifying men's taste, as it modifies their manners and their pleasures. This, he contends, is what all great workmen had always understood. Dante,[5] Shakespeare, Molière, had exercised an absolute independence in their choice of subject and treatment. To turn always with that ever-changing spirit, yet to retain the flavour of what was admirably done in past generations, in the classics, as we say—is the problem of true romanticism. 'Dante', he observes, 'was pre-eminently the romantic poet. He adored Virgil, yet he wrote the *Divine Comedy*, with the episode of Ugolino, which is as unlike the *Æneid* as can possibly be. And those who thus obey the fundamental principle of romanticism, one by one become classical, and are joined

to that ever-increasing common league, formed by men of all
countries, to approach nearer and nearer to perfection.'

Romanticism, then, although it has its epochs, is in its essential
characteristics rather a spirit which shows itself at all times, in various
degrees, in individual workmen and their work, and the amount of
which criticism has to estimate in them taken one by one, than the
peculiarity of a time or a school. Depending on the varying proportion of curiosity and the desire of beauty, natural tendencies of the
artistic spirit at all times, it must always be partly a matter of individual temperament. The eighteenth century in England has been
regarded as almost exclusively a classical period; yet William Blake,
a type of so much which breaks through what are conventionally
thought the influences of that century, is still a noticeable phenomenon in it, and the reaction in favour of naturalism in poetry begins
in that century, early. There are, thus, the born romanticists and the
born classicists. There are the born classicists who start with *form*, to
whose minds the comeliness of the old, immemorial, well-recognized
types in art and literature, have revealed themselves impressively;
who will entertain no matter which will not go easily and flexibly
into them; whose work aspires only to be a variation upon, or study
from, the older masters. ''Tis art's decline, my son!' they are always
saying, to the progressive element in their own generation; to those
who care for that which in fifty years' time every one will be caring
for. On the other hand, there are the born romanticists, who start
with an original, untried *matter*, still in fusion; who conceive this
vividly, and hold by it as the essence of their work; who, by the very
vividness and heat of their conception, purge away, sooner or later, all
that is not organically appropriate to it, till the whole effect adjusts
itself in clear, orderly, proportionate form; which form, after a very
little time, becomes classical in its turn.

The romantic or classical character of a picture, a poem, a literary
work, depends, then, on the balance of certain qualities in it; and in
this sense, a very real distinction may be drawn between good classical
and good romantic work. But all critical terms are relative; and there
is at least a valuable suggestion in that theory of Stendhal's, that all
good art was romantic in its day. In the beauties of Homer and
Pheidias, quiet as they now seem, there must have been, for those who
confronted them for the first time, excitement and surprise, the sudden
unforeseen satisfaction of the desire of beauty. Yet the *Odyssey*, with
its marvellous adventure, is more romantic than the *Iliad*, which
nevertheless contains, among many other romantic episodes, that of
the immortal horses of Achilles, who weep at the death of Patroclus.
Æschylus is more romantic than Sophocles, whose *Philoctetes*, were

it written now, might figure, for the strangeness of its motive and the perfectness of its execution, as typically romantic; while, of Euripides, it may be said, that his method in writing his plays is to sacrifice readily almost everything else, so that he may attain the fulness of a single romantic effect. These two tendencies, indeed, might be applied as a measure or standard, all through Greek and Roman art and poetry, with very illuminating results; and for an analyst of the romantic principle in art, no exercise would be more profitable, than to walk through the collection of classical antiquities at the Louvre, or the British Museum, or to examine some representative collection of Greek coins, and note how the element of curiosity, of the love of strangeness, insinuates itself into classical design, and record the effects of the romantic spirit there, the traces of struggle, of the grotesque even, though over-balanced here by sweetness; as in the sculpture of Chartres and Rheims, the real sweetness of mind in the sculptor is often overbalanced by the grotesque, by the rudeness of his strength.

Classicism, then, means for Stendhal, for that younger enthusiastic band of French writers whose unconscious method he formulated into principles, the reign of what is pedantic, conventional, and narrowly academical in art; for him, all good art is romantic. To Sainte-Beuve, who understands the term in a more liberal sense, it is the characteristic of certain epochs, of certain spirits in every epoch, not given to the exercise of original imagination, but rather to the working out of refinements of manner on some authorised matter; and who bring to their perfection, in this way, the elements of sanity, of order and beauty in manner. In general criticism, again, it means the spirit of Greece and Rome, of some phases in literature and art that may seem of equal authority with Greece and Rome, the age of Louis the Fourteenth, the age of Johnson; though this is at best an uncritical use of the term, because in Greek and Roman work there are typical examples of the romantic spirit. But explain the terms as we may, in application to particular epochs, there are these two elements always recognisable; united in perfect art—in Sophocles, in Dante, in the highest work of Goethe, though not always absolutely balanced there; and these two elements may be not inappropriately termed the classical and romantic tendencies.

Material for the artist, motives of inspiration, are not yet exhausted: our curious, complex, aspiring age still abounds in subjects for æsthetic manipulation by the literary as well as by other forms of art. For the literary art, at all events, the problem just now is, to induce order upon the contorted, proportionless accumulation of our

knowledge and experience, our science and history, our hopes and
disillusion, and, in effecting this, to do consciously what has been done
hitherto for the most part too unconsciously, to write our English
language as the Latins wrote theirs, as the French write, as scholars
should write. Appealing, as he may, to precedent in this matter, the
scholar will still remember that if 'the style is the man' it is also the
age: that the nineteenth century too will be found to have had its
style, justified by necessity—a style very different, alike from the
baldness of an impossible 'Queen Anne' revival, and an incorrect,
incondite exuberance, after the mode of Elizabeth: that we can only
return to either at the price of an impoverishment of form or matter,
or both, although, an intellectually rich age such as ours being
necessarily an eclectic one, we may well cultivate some of the excellences of literary types so different as those: that in literature as in
other matters it is well to unite as many diverse elements as may be:
that the individual writer or artist, certainly, is to be estimated by
the number of graces he combines, and his power of interpenetrating
them in a given work. To discriminate schools, of art, of literature, is,
of course, part of the obvious business of literary criticism: but, in
the work of literary production, it is easy to be overmuch occupied
concerning them. For, in truth, the legitimate contention is, not of
one age or school of literary art against another, but of all successive
schools alike, against the stupidity which is dead to the substance, and
the vulgarity which is dead to form.

THE MARBLES OF ÆGINA[1]

I have dwelt the more emphatically upon the purely sensuous aspects of early Greek art, on the beauty and charm of its mere material and workmanship, the grace of hand in it, its chryselephantine character, because the direction of all the more general criticism since Lessing has been, somewhat one-sidedly, towards the ideal or abstract element in Greek art, towards what we may call its philosophical aspect.[2] And, indeed, this philosophical element, a tendency to the realisation of a certain inward, abstract, intellectual ideal, is also at work in Greek art—a tendency which, if that chryselephantine influence is called Ionian, may rightly be called the Dorian, or, in reference to its broader scope, the European influence; and this European influence or tendency is really towards the impression of an order, a sanity, a proportion in all work, which shall reflect the inward order of human reason, now fully conscious of itself,—towards a sort of art in which the record and delineation of humanity, as active in the wide, inward world of its passion and thought, has become more or less definitely the aim of all artistic handicraft.

In undergoing the action of these two opposing influences, and by harmonising in itself their antagonism, Greek sculpture does but reflect the larger movements of more general Greek history. All through Greek history we may trace, in every sphere of the activity of the Greek mind, the action of these two opposing tendencies,—the centrifugal and centripetal tendencies, as we may perhaps not too fancifully call them. There is the centrifugal, the Ionian, the Asiatic tendency, flying from the centre, working with little forethought straight before it, in the development of every thought and fancy; throwing itself forth in endless play of undirected imagination; delighting in brightness and colour, in beautiful material, in change-ful form everywhere, in poetry, in philosophy, even in architecture and its subordinate crafts. In the social and political order it rejoices in the freest action of local and personal influences; its restless versatility drives it towards the assertion of the principles of separatism, of individualism,—the separation of state from state, the maintenance of local religions, the development of the individual in that which is most peculiar and individual in him. Its claim is in its grace, its freedom and happiness, its lively interest, the variety of its gifts to civilisation; its weakness is self-evident, and was what made the unity of Greece impossible. It is this centrifugal tendency which Plato is desirous to cure, by maintaining, over against it, the Dorian influence of a severe simplification everywhere, in society, in culture, in the very physical nature of man. An enemy everywhere to *variegation*, to what is cunning or 'myriad-minded', he sets himself, in mythology, in music, in poetry, in every kind of art, to enforce the ideal of a sort of Parmenidean abstractness and calm.

This exaggerated ideal of Plato's is, however, only the exaggeration of the salutary European tendency, which, finding human mind the most absolutely real and precious thing in the world, enforces everywhere the impress of its sanity, its profound reflexions upon things as they really are, its sense of proportion. It is the centripetal tendency, which links individuals to each other, states to states, one period of organic growth to another, under the reign of a composed, rational, self-conscious order, in the universal light of the understanding.[3]

... To that Asiatic tradition, then, with its perfect craftsmanship, its consummate skill in design, its power of hand, the Dorian, the European, the true Hellenic influence brought a revelation of the soul and body of man.

STYLE [1]

Since all progress of mind consists for the most part in differentiation, in the resolution of an obscure and complex object into its component aspects, it is surely the stupidest of losses to confuse things which right reason has put asunder, to lose the sense of achieved distinctions, the distinction between poetry and prose, for instance, or, to speak more exactly, between the laws and characteristic excellences of verse and prose composition. On the other hand, those who have dwelt most emphatically on the distinction between prose and verse, prose and poetry, may sometimes have been tempted to limit the proper functions of prose too narrowly; and this again is at least false economy, as being, in effect, the renunciation of a certain means or faculty, in a world where after all we must needs make the most of things.[2] Critical efforts to limit art *a priori*, by anticipations regarding the natural incapacity of the material with which this or that artist works, as the sculptor with solid form, or the prose-writer with the ordinary language of men, are always liable to be discredited by the facts of artistic production; and while prose is actually found to be a coloured thing with Bacon, picturesque with Livy and Carlyle, musical with Cicero and Newman, mystical and intimate with Plato and Michelet and Sir Thomas Browne, exalted or florid, it may be, with Milton and Taylor,[3] it will be useless to protest that it can be nothing at all, except something very tamely and narrowly confined to mainly practical ends—a kind of 'good round-hand'; as useless as the protest that poetry might not touch prosaic subjects as with Wordsworth, or an abstruse matter as with Browning, or treat contemporary life nobly as with Tennyson. In subordination to one essential beauty in all good literary style, in all literature as a fine art, as there are many beauties of poetry so the beauties of prose are many, and it is the business of criticism to estimate them as such; as it is good in the criticism of verse to look for those hard, logical, and quasi-prosaic excellences which that too has, or needs. To find in the poem, amid the flowers, the allusions, the mixed perspectives, of *Lycidas* for instance, the thought, the logical structure:—how wholesome! how delightful! as to identify in prose what we call the poetry, the imaginative power, not treating it as out of place and a kind of vagrant intruder, but by way of an estimate of its rights, that is, of its achieved powers, there.

Dryden, with the characteristic instinct of his age, loved to emphasise the distinction between poetry and prose, the protest against their confusion with each other, coming with somewhat diminished effect from one whose poetry was so prosaic. In truth, his sense of prosaic excellence affected his verse rather than his prose, which is not only fervid, richly figured, poetic, as we say, but vitiated, all unconsciously, by many a scanning line. Setting up correctness, that humble merit of prose, as the central literary excellence, he is really a less correct writer than he may seem, still with an imperfect mastery of the relative pronoun. It might have been foreseen that, in the rotations of mind, the province of poetry in prose would find its assertor; and, a century after Dryden, amid very different intellectual needs, and with the need therefore of great modifications in literary form, the range of the poetic force in literature was effectively enlarged by Wordsworth. The true distinction between prose and poetry he regarded as the almost technical or accidental one of the absence or presence of metrical beauty, or, say! metrical restraint; and for him the opposition came to be between verse and prose of course; but, as the essential dichotomy in this matter, between imaginative and unimaginative writing, parallel to De Quincey's distinction between 'the literature of power and the literature of knowledge',[4] in the former of which the composer gives us not fact, but his peculiar sense of fact, whether past or present.

Dismissing then, under sanction of Wordsworth, that harsher opposition of poetry to prose, as savouring in fact of the arbitrary psychology of the last century, and with it the prejudice that there can be but one only beauty of prose style, I propose here to point out certain qualities of all literature as a fine art, which, if they apply to the literature of fact, apply still more to the literature of the imaginative sense of fact, while they apply indifferently to verse and prose, so far as either is really imaginative—certain conditions of true art in both alike, which conditions may also contain in them the secret of the proper discrimination and guardianship of the peculiar excellences of either.

The line between fact and something quite different from external fact is, indeed, hard to draw. In Pascal,[5] for instance, in the persuasive writers generally, how difficult to define the point where, from time to time, argument which, if it is to be worth anything at all, must consist of facts or groups of facts, becomes a pleading—a theorem no longer, but essentially an appeal to the reader to catch the writer's spirit, to think with him, if one can or will—an expression no longer of fact but of his sense of it, his peculiar intuition of a world, prospective, or discerned below the faulty conditions of the present, in either case changed somewhat from the actual world. In science, on the other hand, in history so far as it conforms to scientific rule, we have a literary domain where the imagination may be thought to be always an intruder. And as, in all science, the functions of literature reduce themselves eventually to the transcribing of fact, so all the excellences of literary form in regard to science are reducible to various kinds of painstaking; this good quality being involved in all 'skilled work' whatever, in the drafting of an act of parliament, as in sewing. Yet here again, the writer's sense of fact, in history especially, and in all those complex subjects which do but lie on the borders of science, will still take the place of fact, in various degrees. Your historian, for instance, with absolutely truthful intention, amid the multitude of facts presented to him must needs select, and in selecting assert something of his own humour, something that comes not of the world without but of a vision within. So Gibbon moulds his unwieldy material to a preconceived view. Livy, Tacitus, Michelet, moving full of poignant sensibility amid the records of the past, each, after his own sense, modifies—who can tell where and to what degree?—and becomes something else than a transcriber; each, as he thus modifies, passing into the domain of art proper. For just in proportion as the writer's aim, consciously or unconsciously, comes to be the transcribing, not of the world, not of mere fact, but of his sense of it, he becomes an artist, his work *fine* art; and good art (as I hope ultimately to show) in proportion to the truth of his presentment of that sense; as in those humbler or plainer functions of literature also, truth—truth to bare fact, there—is the essence of such artistic quality as they may have. Truth! there can be no merit, no craft at all, without that. And further, all beauty is in the long run only *fineness* of truth, or what we call expression, the finer accommodation of speech to that vision within.

—The transcript of his sense of fact rather than the fact, as being preferable, pleasanter, more beautiful to the writer himself. In literature, as in every other product of human skill, in the moulding of a bell or a platter for instance, wherever this sense asserts itself, wherever the producer so modifies his work as, over and above its primary use or intention, to make it pleasing (to himself, of course, in the first instance) there, 'fine' as opposed to merely serviceable art, exists. Literary art, that is, like all art which is in any way imitative or reproductive of fact—form, or colour, or incident—is the representation of such fact as connected with soul, of a specific personality, in its preferences, its volition and power.

Such is the matter of imaginative or artistic literature—this transcript, not of mere fact, but of fact in its infinite variety, as modified by human preference in all its infinitely varied forms. It will be good literary art not because it is brilliant or sober, or rich, or impulsive, or severe, but just in proportion as its representation of that sense, that soul-fact, is true, verse being only one department of such literature, and imaginative prose, it may be thought, being the special art of the modern world.[6] That imaginative prose should be the special and opportune art of the modern world results from two important facts about the latter: first, the chaotic variety and complexity of its interests, making the intellectual issue, the really master currents of the present time incalculable—a condition of mind little susceptible of the restraint proper to verse form, so that the most characteristic verse of the nineteenth century has been lawless verse; and secondly, an all-pervading naturalism, a curiosity about everything whatever as it really is, involving a certain humility of attitude, cognate to what must, after all, be the less ambitious form of literature. And prose thus asserting itself as the special and priviliged artistic faculty of the present day, will be, however critics may try to narrow its scope, as varied in its excellence as humanity itself reflecting on the facts of its latest experience—an instrument of many stops, meditative, observant descriptive, eloquent, analytic, plaintive, fervid. Its beauties will be not exclusively 'pedestrian': it will exert, in due measure, all the varied charms of poetry, down to the rhythm which, as in Cicero, or Michelet, or Newman, at their best, gives its musical value to every syllable.*

The literary artist is of necessity a scholar, and in what he proposes to do will have in mind, first of all, the scholar and the scholarly conscience—the male conscience in this matter, as we must think it, under a system of education which still to so large an extent limits real scholarship to men. In his self-criticism, he supposes always that sort of reader who will go (full of eyes) warily, considerately, though without consideration for him, over the ground which the female conscience traverses so lightly, so amiably. For the material in which

---

* Mr Saintsbury, in his *Specimens of English Prose, from Malory to Macaulay*, has succeeded in tracing, through successive English prose-writers, the tradition of that severer beauty in them, of which this admirable scholar of our literature is known to be a lover.[7] *English Prose, from Mandeville to Thackeray*, more recently 'chosen and edited' by a younger scholar, Mr Arthur Galton, of New College, Oxford, a lover of our literature at once enthusiastic and discreet, aims at a more various illustration of the eloquent powers of English prose, and is a delightful companion.

he works is no more a creation of his own than the sculptor's marble. Product of a myriad various minds and contending tongues, compact of obscure and minute association, a language has its own abundant and often recondite laws, in the habitual and summary recognition of which scholarship consists. A writer, full of a matter he is before all things anxious to express, may think of those laws, the limitations of vocabulary, structure, and the like, as a restriction, but if a real artist will find in them an opportunity. His punctilious observance of the proprieties of his medium will diffuse through all he writes a general air of sensibility, of refined usage. *Exclusiones debitæ naturæ*—the exclusions, or rejections, which nature demands—we know how large a part they play, according to Bacon, in the science of nature. In a somewhat changed sense, we might say that the art of the scholar is summed up in the observance of those rejections demanded by the nature of his medium, the material he must use. Alive to the value of an atmosphere in which every term finds its utmost degree of expression, and with all the jealousy of a lover of words, he will resist a constant tendency on the part of the majority of those who use them to efface the distinctions of language, the facility of writers often reinforcing in this respect the work of the vulgar. He will feel the obligation not of the laws only, but of those affinities, avoidances, those mere preferences, of his language, which through the associations of literary history have become a part of its nature, prescribing the rejection of many a neology, many a license, many a gipsy phrase which might present itself as actually expressive. His appeal, again, is to the scholar, who has great experience in literature, and will show no favour to short-cuts, or hackneyed illustration, or an affectation of learning designed for the unlearned. [Hence a contention, a sense of self-restraint and renunciation, having for the susceptible reader the effect of a challenge for minute consideration; the attention of the writer, in every minutest detail, being a pledge that it is worth the reader's while to be attentive too, that the writer is dealing scrupulously with his instrument, and therefore, indirectly, with the reader himself also, that he has the science of the instrument he plays on, perhaps, after all, with a freedom which in such case will be the freedom of a master.]

For meanwhile, braced only by those restraints, he is really vindicating his liberty in the making of a vocabulary, an entire system of composition, for himself, his own true manner; and when we speak of the manner of a true master we mean what is essential in his art. Pedantry being only the scholarship of *le cuistre* (we have no English equivalent) he is no pedant, and does but show his intelligence of the rules of language in his freedoms with it, addition or expansion, which like the spontaneities of manner in a well-bred person will still further illustrate good taste.—The right vocabulary! Translators have not invariably seen how all-important that is in the work of translation, driving for the most part at idiom or construction; whereas, if the original be first-rate, one's first care should be with its elementary particles, Plato, for instance, being often reproducible by an exact following, with no variation in structure, of word after word, as the pencil follows a drawing under tracing-paper, so only each word or syllable be not of false colour, to change my illustration a little.

Well! that is because any writer worth translating at all has winnowed and searched through his vocabulary, is conscious of the words he would select in systematic reading of a dictionary, and still more of the words he would reject were the dictionary other than Johnson's; and doing this with his peculiar sense of the world ever in view, in search of an instrument for the adequate expression of that, he begets a vocabulary faithful to the colouring of his own spirit, and in the strictest sense original. That living authority which language needs lies, in truth, in its scholars, who recognising always that every language possesses a genius, a very fastidious genius, of its own, expand at once and purify its very elements, which must needs change along with the changing thoughts of living people. Ninety years ago, for instance, great mental force, certainly, was needed by Wordsworth, to break through the consecrated poetic associations of a century, and speak the language that was his, that was to become in a measure the language of the next generation. But he did it with the tact of a scholar also. English, for a quarter of a century past, has been assimilating the phraseology of pictorial art; for half a century, the phraseology of the great German metaphysical movement of eighty years ago; in part also the language of mystical theology: and none but pedants will regret a great consequent increase of its resources. For many years to come its enterprise may well lie in the naturalisation of the vocabulary of science, so only it be under the eye of a sensitive scholarship—in a liberal naturalisation of the ideas of science too, for after all the chief stimulus of good style is to possess a full, rich, complex matter to grapple with. The literary artist, therefore, will be well aware of physical science; science also attaining, in its turn, its true literary ideal. And then, as the scholar is nothing without the historic sense, he will be apt to restore not really obsolete or really worn-out words, but the finer edge of words still in use: *ascertain, communicate, discover*—words like these it has been part of our 'business' to misuse. And still, as language was made for man, he will be no authority for correctnesses which, limiting freedom of utterance, were yet but accidents in their origin; as if one vowed not to say '*its*', which ought to have been in Shakespeare; '*his*' and '*hers*', for inanimate objects, being but a barbarous and really inexpressive survival. Yet we have known many things like this. Racy Saxon monosyllables, close to us as touch and sight, he will intermix readily with those long, savoursome, Latin words, rich in 'second intention'. In this late day certainly, no critical process can be conducted reasonably without eclecticism. Of such eclecticism we have a justifying example in one of the first poets of our time. How illustrative of monosyllabic effect, of sonorous Latin, of the phraseology of science, of metaphysic, of colloquialism even, are the writings of Tennyson; yet with what a fine, fastidious scholarship throughout!

A scholar writing for the scholarly, he will of course leave something to the willing intelligence of his reader. 'To go preach to the first passer-by', says Montaigne, 'to become tutor to the ignorance of the first I meet, is a thing I abhor'; a thing, in fact, naturally distressing to the scholar, who will therefore ever be shy of offering uncomplimentary assistance to the reader's wit. To really strenuous minds there is a pleasurable stimulus in the challenge for a continuous effort on their part, to be rewarded by securer and more intimate grasp of the author's sense. Self-restraint, a skilful economy of means, *ascêsis*, that too has a beauty of its own; and for the reader supposed there will be an æsthetic satisfaction in that frugal closeness of style which makes the most of a word, in the exaction from every sentence of a precise relief, in the just spacing out of word to thought, in the logically filled space connected always with the delightful sense of difficulty overcome.

Different classes of persons, at different times, make, of course, very various demands upon literature. Still, scholars, I suppose, and not only scholars, but all disinterested lovers of books, will always look to it, as to all other fine art, for a refuge, a sort of cloistral refuge, from a certain vulgarity in the actual world. A perfect poem like *Lycidas*, a perfect fiction like *Esmond*, the perfect handling of a theory like Newman's *Idea of a University*, has for them something of the uses of a religious 'retreat'. Here, then, with a view to the central need of a select few, those 'men of a finer thread' who have formed and maintain the literary ideal, everything, every component element, will have undergone exact trial, and, above all, there will be no uncharacteristic or tarnished or vulgar decoration, permissible ornament being for the most part structural, or necessary. As the painter in his picture, so the artist in his book, aims at the production by honourable artifice of a peculiar atmosphere. 'The artist', says Schiller, 'may be known rather by what he *omits*'; and in literature, too, the true artist may be best recognised by his tact of omission. For to the grave reader words too are grave; and the ornamental word, the figure, the accessory form or colour or reference, is rarely content to die to thought precisely at the right moment, but will inevitably linger awhile, stirring a long 'brainwave' behind it of perhaps quite alien associations.

Just there, it may be, is the detrimental tendency of the sort of scholarly attentiveness of mind I am recommending.[8] But the true artist allows for it. He will remember that, as the very word ornament indicates what is in itself non-essential, so the 'one beauty' of all literary style is of its very essence, and independent, in prose and verse alike, of all removable decoration; that it may exist in its fullest lustre, as in Flaubert's *Madame Bovary*, for instance, or in Stendhal's *Le Rouge et Le Noir*, in a composition utterly unadorned, with hardly a single suggestion of visibly beautiful things. Parallel, allusion, the allusive way generally, the flowers in the garden:—he knows the narcotic force of these upon the negligent intelligence to which any *diversion*, literally, is welcome, any vagrant intruder, because one can go wandering away with it from the immediate subject. Jealous, if he have a really quickening motive within, of all that does not hold directly to that, of the facile, the otiose, he will never depart from the strictly pedestrian process, unless he gains a ponderable something thereby. Even assured of its congruity, he will still question its serviceableness. Is it worth while, can we afford, to attend to just that, to just that figure or literary reference, just then?—Surplusage! he will dread that, as the runner on his muscles. For in truth all art does but consist in the removal of surplusage, from the last finish of the gem-engraver blowing away the last particle of invisible dust, back to the earliest divination of the finished work to be, lying somewhere, according to Michelangelo's fancy, in the rough-hewn block of stone.

And what applies to figure or flower must be understood of all other accidental or removable ornaments of writing whatever; and not of specific ornament only, but of all that latent colour and imagery which language as such carries in it. A lover of words for their own sake, to whom nothing about them is unimportant, a minute and constant observer of their physiognomy, he will be on the alert not only for obviously mixed metaphors of course, but for the metaphor that is mixed in all our speech, though a rapid use may involve no cognition of it. Currently recognising the incident, the colour, the physical elements or particles in words like *absorb*, *consider*, *extract*, to take the first that occur, he will avail himself of them, as further adding to the resources of expression. The elementary particles of language will be realised as colour and light and shade through his scholarly living in the full sense of them. Still opposing the constant degradation of language by those who use it carelessly, he will not treat coloured glass as if it were clear; and while half the world is using figure unconsciously, will be fully aware not only of all that latent figurative texture in speech, but of the vague, lazy, half-formed personification—a rhetoric, depressing, and worse than nothing, because it has no really rhetorical motive—which plays so large a part there, and, as in the case of more ostentatious ornament, scrupulously exact of it, from syllable to syllable, its precise value.

So far I have been speaking of certain conditions of the literary art arising out of the medium or material in or upon which it works, the essential qualities of language and its aptitudes for contingent ornamentation, matters which define scholarship as science and good taste respectively. They are both subservient to a more intimate quality of good style: more intimate, as coming nearer to the artist himself. The otiose, the facile, surplusage: why are these abhorrent to the true literary artist, except because, in literary as in all other art, structure is all-important, felt, or painfully missed, everywhere?—that architectural conception of work, which foresees the end in the beginning and never loses sight of it, and in every part is conscious of all the rest, till the last sentence does but, with undiminished vigour, unfold and justify the first—a condition of literary art, which, in contradistinction to another quality of the artist himself, to be spoken of later, I shall call the necessity of *mind* in style.

An acute philosophical writer, the late Dean Mansel (a writer whose works illustrate the literary beauty there may be in closeness, and with obvious repression or economy of a fine rhetorical gift) wrote a book, of fascinating precision in a very obscure subject, to show that all the technical laws of logic are but means of securing, in each and all of its apprehensions, the unity, the strict identity with itself, of the apprehending mind. All the laws of good writing aim at a similar unity or identity of the mind in all the processes by which the word is associated to its import. The term is right, and has its essential beauty, when it becomes, in a manner, what it signifies, as with the names of simple sensations. To give the phrase, the sentence, the structural member, the entire composition, song, or essay, a similar unity with its subject and with itself:—style is in the right way when it tends towards that. All depends upon the original unity, the vital wholeness and identity, of the initiatory apprehension or view. So much is true of all art, which therefore requires always its logic, its comprehensive reason—insight, foresight, retrospect, in simultaneous action—true, most of all, of the literary art, as being of all the arts most closely cognate to the abstract intelligence. Such logical coherency may be evidenced not merely in the lines of composition as a whole, but in the

choice of a single word, while it by no means interferes with, but may
even prescribe, much variety, in the building of the sentence for
instance, or in the manner, argumentative, descriptive, discursive, of
this or that part or member of the entire design. The blithe, crisp
sentence, decisive as a child's expression of its needs, may alternate
with the long-contending, victoriously intricate sentence; the
sentence, born with the integrity of a single word, relieving the sort
of sentence in which, if you look closely, you can see much contrivance,
much adjustment, to being a highly qualified matter into compass at
one view. For the literary architecture, if it is to be rich and expressive,
involves not only foresight of the end in the beginning, but also
development or growth of design, in the process of execution, with
many irregularities, surprises, and afterthoughts; the contingent as
well as the necessary being subsumed under the unity of the whole.
As truly, to the lack of such architectural design, of a single, almost
visual, image, vigorously informing an entire, perhaps very intricate,
composition, which shall be austere, ornate, argumentative, fanciful,
yet true from first to last to that vision within, may be attributed those
weaknesses of conscious or unconscious repetition of word, phrase,
motive, or member of the whole matter, indicating, as Flaubert was
aware, an original structure in thought not organically complete.
With such foresight, the actual conclusion will most often get itself
written out of hand, before, in the more obvious sense, the work is
finished. With some strong and leading sense of the world, the tight
hold of which secures true *composition* and not mere loose accretion,
the literary artist, I suppose, goes on considerately, setting joint to
joint, sustained by yet restraining the productive ardour, retracing
the negligences of his first sketch, repeating his steps only that he may
give the reader a sense of secure and restful progress, readjusting mere
assonances even, that they may soothe the reader, or at least not in-
terrupt him on his way; and then, somewhere before the end comes,
is burdened, inspired, with his conclusion, and betimes delivered of it,
leaving off, not in weariness and because he finds *himself* at an end,
but in all the freshness of volition. His work now structurally complete,
with all the accumulating effect of secondary shades of meaning, he
finishes the whole up to the just proportion of that ante-penultimate
conclusion, and all becomes expressive. The house he has built is
rather a body he has informed. And so it happens, to its greater
credit, that the better interest even of a narrative to be recounted, a
story to be told, will often be in its second reading. And though there
are instances of great writers who have been no artists, an unconscious tact sometimes directing work in which we may detect,
very pleasurably, many of the effects of conscious art, yet one of the

greatest pleasures of really good prose literature is in the critical tracing out of that conscious artistic structure, and the pervading sense of it as we read. Yet of poetic literature too; for, in truth, the kind of constructive intelligence here supposed is one of the forms of the imagination.

That is the special function of mind, in style. Mind and soul:— hard to ascertain philosophically, the distinction is real enough practically, for they often interfere, are sometimes in conflict, with each other. Blake, in the last century, is an instance of preponderating soul, embarrassed, at a loss, in an era of preponderating mind. As a quality of style, at all events, soul is a fact, in certain writers—the way they have of absorbing language, of attracting it into the peculiar spirit they are of, with a subtlety which makes the actual result seem like some inexplicable inspiration. By mind, the literary artist reaches us, through static and objective indications of design in his work, legible to all. By soul, he reaches us, somewhat capriciously perhaps, one and not another, through vagrant sympathy and a kind of immediate contact. Mind we cannot choose but approve where we recognise it; soul may repel us, not because we misunderstand it. The way in which theological interests sometimes avail themselves of language is perhaps the best illustration of the force I mean to indicate generally in literature, by the word *soul*. Ardent religious persuasion may exist, may make its way, without finding any equivalent heat in language: or, again, it may enkindle words to various degrees, and when it really takes hold of them doubles its force. Religious history presents many remarkable instances in which, through no mere phrase-worship, an unconscious literary tact has, for the sensitive, laid open a privileged pathway from one to another. 'The altar-fire', people say, 'has touched those lips!' The Vulgate, the English Bible, the English Prayer-Book, the writings of Swedenborg, the Tracts for the Times:—there, we have instances of widely different and largely diffused phases of religious feeling in operation as soul in style. But something of the same kind acts with similar power in certain writers of quite other than theological literature, on behalf of some wholly personal and peculiar sense of theirs. Most easily illustrated by theological literature, this quality lends to profane writers a kind of religious influence. At their best, these writers become, as we say sometimes, 'prophets'; such character depending on the effect not merely of their matter, but of their matter as allied to, in 'electric affinity' with, peculiar form, and working in all cases by an immediate sympathetic contact, on which account it is that it may be called soul, as opposed to mind, in style. And this too is a faculty of choosing and rejecting what is congruous or otherwise, with a drift towards unity—

unity of atmosphere here, as there of design—soul securing colour (or perfume, might we say?) as mind secures form, the latter being essentially finite, the former vague or infinite, as the influence of a living person is practically infinite. There are some to whom nothing has any real interest, or real meaning, except as operative in a given person; and it is they who best appreciate the quality of soul in literary art. They seem to know a *person*, in a book, and make way by intuition: yet, although they thus enjoy the completeness of a personal information, it is still a characteristic of soul, in this sense of the word, that it does but suggest what can never be uttered, not as being different from, or more obscure than, what actually gets said, but as containing that plenary substance of which there is only one phase or facet in what is there expressed.

If all high things have their martyrs, Gustave Flaubert might perhaps rank as the martyr of literary style.[9] In his printed correspondence, a curious series of letters, written in his twenty-fifth year, records what seems to have been his one other passion—a series of letters which, with its fine casuistries, its firmly repressed anguish, its tone of harmonious grey, and the sense of disillusion in which the whole matter ends, might have been, a few slight changes supposed, one of his own fictions. Writing to Madame X. certainly he does display, by 'taking thought' mainly, by constant and delicate pondering, as in his love for literature, a heart really moved, but still more, and as the pledge of that emotion, a loyalty to his work. Madame X., too, is a literary artist, and the best gifts he can send her are precepts of perfection in art, counsels for the effectual pursuit of that better love. In his love-letters it is the pains and pleasures of art he insists on, its solaces: he communicates secrets, reproves, encourages, with a view to that. Whether the lady was dissatisfied with such divided or indirect service, the reader is not enabled to see; but sees that, on Flaubert's part at least, a living person could be no rival of what was, from first to last, his leading passion, a somewhat solitary and exclusive one.

I must scold you (he writes) for one thing, which shocks, scandalises me, the small concern, namely, you show for art just now. As regards glory be it so: there, I approve. But for art!—the one thing in life that is good and real —can you compare with it an earthly love?—prefer the adoration of a relative beauty to the *cultus* of the true beauty? Well! I tell you the truth. That is the one thing good in me: the one thing I have, to me estimable. For yourself, you blend with the beautiful a heap of alien things, the useful, the agreeable, what not?—

The only way not to be unhappy is to shut yourself up in art, and count everything else as nothing. Pride takes the place of all beside when it is established on a large basis. Work! God wills it. That, it seems to me, is clear.—

I am reading over again the *Æneid*, certain verses of which I repeat to myself to satiety. There are phrases there which stay in one's head, by which I find myself beset, as with those musical airs which are for ever returning, and cause you pain, you love them so much. I observe that I no longer laugh much, and am no longer depressed. I am ripe. You talk of my serenity, and envy me. It may well surprise you. Sick, irritated, the prey a thousand times a day of cruel pain, I continue my labour like a true working-man, who, with sleeves turned up, in the sweat of his brow, beats away at his anvil, never troubling himself whether it rains or blows, for hail or thunder. I was not like that formerly. The change has taken place naturally, though my will has counted for something in the matter.—

Those who write in good style are sometimes accused of a neglect of ideas, and of the moral end, as if the end of the physician were something else than healing, of the painter than painting—as if the end of art were not, before all else, the beautiful.

What, then, did Flaubert understand by beauty, in the art he pursued with so much fervour, with so much self-command? Let us hear a sympathetic commentator :—

Possessed of an absolute belief that there exists but one way of expressing one thing, one word to call it by, one adjective to qualify, one verb to animate it, he gave himself to super-human labour for the discovery, in every phrase, of that word, that verb, that epithet. In this way, he believed in some mysterious harmony of expression, and when a true word seemed to him to lack euphony still went on seeking another, with invincible patience, certain that he had not yet got hold of the *unique* word. . . . A thousand preoccupations would beset him at the same moment, always with this desperate certitude fixed in his spirit: Among all the expressions in the world, all forms and turns of expression, there is but *one*—one form, one mode—to express what I want to say.

The one word for the one thing, the one thought, amid the multitude of words, terms, that might just do: the problem of style was there!—the unique word, phrase, sentence, paragraph, essay, or song, absolutely proper to the single mental presentation or vision within. In that perfect justice, over and above the many contingent and removable beauties with which beautiful style may charm us, but which it can exist without, independent of them yet dexterously availing itself of them, omnipresent in good work, in function at every point, from single epithets to the rhythm of a whole book, lay the specific, indispensable, very intellectual, beauty of literature, the possibility of which constitutes it a fine art.

One seems to detect the influence of a philosophic idea there, the idea of a natural economy, of some pre-existent adaptation, between a relative, somewhere in the world of thought, and its correlative, somewhere in the world of language—both alike, rather, somewhere in the mind of the artist, desiderative, expectant, inventive—meeting each other with the readiness of 'soul and body reunited', in Blake's rapturous design; and, in fact, Flaubert was fond of giving his theory philosophical expression.—

There are no beautiful thoughts (he would say) without beautiful forms, and conversely. As it is impossible to extract from a physical body the qualities which really constitute it—colour, extension, and the like—without reducing it to a hollow abstraction, in a word, without destroying it; just so it is impossible to detach the form from the idea, for the idea only exists by virtue of the form.

All the recognised flowers, the removable ornaments of literature (including harmony and ease in reading aloud, very carefully considered by him) counted, certainly; for these too are part of the actual value of what one says. But still, after all, with Flaubert, the search, the unwearied research, was not for the smooth, or winsome, or forcible word, as such, as with false Ciceronians, but quite simply and honestly, for the word's adjustment to its meaning. The first condition of this must be, of course, to know yourself, to have ascertained your own sense exactly. Then, if we suppose an artist, he says to the reader,—I want you to see precisely what I see. Into the mind sensitive to 'form', a flood of random sounds, colours, incidents, is ever penetrating from the world without, to become, by sympathetic selection, a part of its very structure, and, in turn, the visible vesture and expression of that other world it sees so steadily within, nay, already with a partial conformity thereto, to be refined, enlarged, corrected, at a hundred points; and it is just there, just at those doubtful points that the function of style, as tact or taste, intervenes. The unique term will come more quickly to one than another, at one time than another, according also to the kind of matter in question. Quickness and slowness, ease and closeness alike, have nothing to do with the artistic character of the true word found at last. As there is a charm of ease, so there is also a special charm in the signs of discovery, of effort and contention towards a due end, as so often with Flaubert himself—in the style which has been pliant, as only obstinate, durable metal can be, to the inherent perplexities and recusancy of a certain difficult thought.

If Flaubert had not told us, perhaps we should never have guessed how tardy and painful his own procedure really was, and after reading his confession may think that his almost endless hesitation had much to do with diseased nerves. Often, perhaps, the felicity supposed will be the product of a happier, a more exuberant nature than Flaubert's. Aggravated, certainly, by a morbid physical condition, that anxiety in 'seeking the phrase', which gathered all the other small *ennuis* of a really quiet existence into a kind of battle, was connected with his lifelong contention against facile poetry, facile art—art, facile and flimsy; and what constitutes the true artist is not the slowness or quickness of the process, but the absolute success of the result. As with those labourers in the parable, the prize is independent of the mere length of the actual day's work. 'You talk', he writes, odd, trying lover, to Madame X.—

'You talk of the exclusiveness of my literary tastes. That might have enabled you to divine what kind of a person I am in the matter of love. I grow so hard to please as a literary artist, that I am driven to despair. I shall end by not writing another line'.

'Happy', he cries, in a moment of discouragement at that patient labour, which for him, certainly, was the condition of a great success—

Happy those who have no doubts of themselves! who lengthen out, as the pen runs on, all that flows forth from their brains. As for me, I hesitate, I disappoint myself, turn round upon myself in despite: my taste is augmented in proportion as my natural vigour decreases, and I afflict my soul over some dubious word out of all proportion to the pleasure I get from a whole page of good writing. One would have to live two centuries to attain a true idea of any matter whatever. What Buffon said is a big blasphemy: genius is not long-continued patience. Still, there is some truth in the statement, and more than people think, especially as regards our own day. Art! art! art! bitter deception! phantom that glows with light, only to lead one on to destruction.

Again—

I am growing so peevish about my writing. I am like a man whose ear is true but who plays falsely on the violin: his fingers refuse to reproduce precisely those sounds of which he has the inward sense. Then the tears come rolling down from the poor scraper's eyes and the bow falls from his hand.

Coming slowly or quickly, when it comes, as it came with so much labour of mind, but also with so much lustre, to Gustave Flaubert, this discovery of the word will be, like all artistic success and felicity, incapable of strict analysis: effect of an intuitive condition of mind, it must be recognised by like intuition on the part of the reader, and a sort of immediate sense. In every one of those masterly sentences of Flaubert there was, below all mere contrivance, shaping and after-thought, by some happy instantaneous concourse of the various faculties of the mind with each other, the exact apprehension of what was *needed* to carry the meaning. And that it fits with absolute justice will be a judgment of immediate sense in the appreciative reader. We all feel this in what may be called inspired translation. Well! all language involves translation from inward to outward. In literature, as in all forms of art, there are the absolute and the merely relative or accessory beauties; and precisely in that exact proportion of the term to its purpose is the absolute beauty of style, prose or verse. All the good qualities, the beauties, of verse also, are such, only as precise expression.

In the highest as in the lowliest literature, then, the one indispensable beauty is, after all, truth:—truth to bare fact in the latter, as to some personal sense of fact, diverted somewhat from men's ordinary sense of it, in the former; truth there as accuracy, truth here as expression, that finest and most intimate form of truth, the *vraie vérité*. And what an eclectic principle this really is! employing for its one sole purpose— that absolute accordance of expression to idea—all other literary beauties and excellences whatever: how many kinds of style it covers, explains, justifies, and at the same time safeguards! Scott's facility, Flaubert's deeply pondered evocation of 'the phrase', are equally good art. Say what you have to say, what you have a will to say, in the simplest, the most direct and exact manner possible, with no surplusage:—there, is the justification of the sentence so fortunately born, 'entire, smooth, and round', that it needs no punctuation, and also (that is the point!) of the most elaborate period, if it be right in its elaboration. Here is the office of ornament: here also the purpose of restraint in ornament. As the exponent of truth, that austerity (the beauty, the function, of which in literature Flaubert understood so well) becomes not the correctness or purism of the mere scholar, but a security against the otiose, a jealous exclusion of what does not really tell towards the pursuit of relief, of life and vigour in the portraiture of one's sense. License again, the making free with rule, if it be indeed, as people fancy, a habit of genius, flinging aside or transforming all that opposes the liberty of beautiful production, will be but faith to one's own meaning. The seeming baldness of *Le Rouge et Le Noir* is nothing in itself; the wild ornament of *Les Misérables* is nothing in itself; and the restraint of Flaubert, amid a real natural opulence, only re-doubled beauty—the phrase so large and so precise at the same time, hard as bronze, in service to the more perfect adaptation of words to their matter. Afterthoughts, retouchings, finish, will be of profit only so far as they too really serve to bring out the original, initiative, generative, sense in them.

In this way, according to the well-known saying, 'The style is the man', complex or simple, in his individuality, his plenary sense of what he really has to say, his sense of the world; all cautions regarding style arising out of so many natural scruples as to the medium through which alone he can expose that inward sense of things, the purity of this medium, its laws or tricks of refraction: nothing is to be left there which might give conveyance to any matter save that. Style in all its varieties, reserved or opulent, terse, abundant, musical, stimulant, academic, so long as each is really characteristic or expressive, finds thus its justification, the sumptuous good taste of Cicero being as truly the man himself, and not another, justified, yet insured inalienably to him, thereby, as would have been his portrait by Raffaelle, in full consular splendour, on his ivory chair.

A relegation, you may say perhaps—a relegation of style to the subjectivity, the mere caprice, of the individual, which must soon transform it into mannerism. Not so! since there is, under the conditions supposed, for those elements of the man, for every lineament of the vision within, the one word, the one acceptable word, recognisable by the sensitive, by others 'who have intelligence' in the matter, as absolutely as ever anything can be in the evanescent and delicate region of human language. The style, the manner, would be the man, not in his unreasoned and really uncharacteristic caprices, involuntary or affected, but in absolutely sincere apprehension of what is most real to him. But let us hear our French guide again.—

Styles (says Flaubert's commentator), *Styles*, as so many peculiar moulds, each of which bears the mark of a particular writer, who is to pour into it the whole content of his ideas, were no part of his theory. What he believed in was *Style*: that is to say, a certain absolute and unique manner of expressing a thing, in all its intensity and colour. For him the *form* was the work itself. As in living creatures, the blood, nourishing the body, determines its very contour and external aspect, just so, to his mind, the *matter*, the basis, in a work of art, imposed, necessarily, the unique, the just expression, the measure, the rhythm—the *form* in all its characteristics.

If the style be the man, in all the colour and intensity of a veritable apprehension, it will be in a real sense 'impersonal'.

I said, thinking of books like Victor Hugo's *Les Misérables*, that prose literature was the characteristic art of the nineteenth century, as others, thinking of its triumphs since the youth of Bach, have assigned that place to music. Music and prose literature are, in one sense, the opposite terms of art; the art of literature presenting to the imagination, through the intelligence, a range of interests, as free and various as those which music presents to it through sense. And certainly the tendency of what has been here said is to bring literature too under those conditions, by conformity to which music takes rank as the typically perfect art. If music be the ideal of all art whatever, precisely because in music it is impossible to distinguish the form from the substance or matter, the subject from the expression, then, literature, by finding its specific excellence in the absolute correspondence of the term to its import, will be but fulfilling the condition of all artistic quality in things everywhere, of all good art.

Good art, but not necessarily great art; the distinction between great art and good art depending immediately, as regards literature at all events, not on its form, but on the matter. Thackeray's *Esmond*, surely, is greater art than *Vanity Fair*, by the greater dignity of its interests. It is on the quality of the matter it informs or controls, its compass, its variety, its alliance to great ends, or the depth of the note of revolt, or the largeness of hope in it, that the greatness of literary art depends, as *The Divine Comedy*, *Paradise Lost*, *Les Misérables*, *The English Bible*, are great art. Given the conditions I have tried to explain as constituting good art;—then, if it be devoted further to the increase of men's happiness, to the redemption of the oppressed, or the enlargement of our sympathies with each other, or to such presentment of new or old truth about ourselves and our relation to the world as may ennoble and fortify us in our sojourn here, or immediately, as with Dante, to the glory of God, it will be also great art; if, over and above those qualities I summed up as mind and soul —that colour and mystic perfume, and that reasonable structure, it has something of the soul of humanity in it, and finds its logical, its architectural place, in the great structure of human life.

Critical Method

Many attempts have been made by writers on art and poetry to define beauty in the abstract, to express it in the most general terms, to find some universal formula for it. The value of these attempts has most often been in the suggestive and penetrating things said by the way. Such discussions help us very little to enjoy what has been well done in art or poetry, to discriminate between what is more and what is less excellent in them, or to use words like beauty, excellence, art, poetry, with a more precise meaning than they would otherwise have. Beauty, like all other qualities presented to human experience, is relative; and the definition of it becomes unmeaning and useless in proportion to its abstractness. To define beauty, not in the most abstract but in the most concrete terms possible, to find not its universal formula, but the formula which expresses most adequately this or that special manifestation of it, is the aim of the true student of æsthetics.

'To see the object as in itself it really is',[1] has been justly said to be the aim of all true criticism whatever; and in æsthetic criticism the first step towards seeing one's object as it really is, is to know one's own impression as it really is, to discriminate it, to realise it distinctly.[2] The objects with which æsthetic criticism deals—music, poetry, artistic and accomplished forms of human life—are indeed receptacles of so many powers or forces: they possess, like the products of nature, so many virtues or qualities. What is this song or picture, this engaging personality presented in life or in a book, to *me?* What effect does it really produce on me? Does it give me pleasure? and if so, what sort or degree of pleasure? How is my nature modified by its presence, and under its influence? The answers to these questions are the original facts with which the æsthetic critic has to do; and, as in the study of light, of morals, of number, one must realise such primary data for one's self, or not at all. And he who experiences these impressions strongly, and drives directly at the discrimination and analysis of them, has no need to trouble himself with the abstract question what beauty is in itself, or what its exact relation to truth or experience—

79

metaphysical questions, as unprofitable as metaphysical questions elsewhere. He may pass them all by as being, answerable or not, of no interest to him.

The æsthetic critic, then, regards all the objects with which he has to do, all works of art, and the fairer forms of nature and human life, as powers or forces producing pleasurable sensations, each of a more or less peculiar or unique kind. This influence he feels, and wishes to explain, by analysing and reducing it to its elements. To him, the picture, the landscape, the engaging personality in life or in a book, *La Gioconda*, the hills of Carrara, Pico of Mirandola, are valuable for their virtues, as we say, in speaking of a herb, a wine, a gem; for the property each has of affecting one with a special, a unique, impression of pleasure. Our education becomes complete in proportion as our susceptibility to these impressions increases in depth and variety. And the function of the æsthetic critic is to distinguish, to analyse, and separate from its adjuncts, the virtue by which a picture, a landscape, a fair personality in life or in a book, produces this special impression of beauty or pleasure, to indicate what the source of that impression is, and under what conditions it is experienced. His end is reached when he has disengaged that virtue, and noted it, as a chemist notes some natural element, for himself and others; and the rule for those who would reach this end is stated with great exactness in the words of a recent critic of Sainte-Beuve:—*De se borner à connaître de près les belles choses, et à s'en nourrir en exquis amateurs, en humanistes accomplis.*

What is important, then, is not that the critic should possess a correct abstract definition of beauty for the intellect, but a certain kind of temperament, the power of being deeply moved by the presence of beautiful objects. He will remember always that beauty exists in many forms. To him all periods, types, schools of taste, are in themselves equal. In all ages there have been some excellent workmen, and some excellent work done. The question he asks is always:—In whom did the stir, the genius, the sentiment of the period find itself? where was the receptacle of its refinement, its elevation, its taste? 'The ages are all equal', says William Blake, 'but genius is always above its age.' [3]

Often it will require great nicety to disengage this virtue from the commoner elements with which it may be found in combination. Few artists, not Goethe or Byron even, work quite cleanly, casting off all *débris*, and leaving us only what the heat of their imagination has wholly fused and transformed. Take, for instance, the writings of Wordsworth. The heat of his genius, entering into the substance of his work, has crystallised a part, but only a part, of it; and in that great mass of verse there is much which might well be forgotten. But scattered up and down it, sometimes fusing and transforming entire compositions, like the Stanzas on *Resolution and Independence*, or the *Ode on the Recollections of Childhood*, sometimes, as if at random, depositing a fine crystal here or there, in a matter it does not wholly search through and transmute, we trace the action of his unique, incommunicable faculty, that strange, mystical sense of a life in natural things, and of man's life as a part of nature, drawing strength and colour and character from local influences, from the hills and streams, and from natural sights and sounds. Well! that is the *virtue*, the active principle in Wordsworth's poetry; and then the function of the critic of Wordsworth is to follow up that active principle, to disengage it, to mark the degree in which it penetrates his verse.[4]

THE GENIUS OF PLATO[1]

All true criticism of philosophic doctrine, as of every other product of human mind, must begin with an historic estimate of the conditions, antecedent and contemporary, which helped to make it precisely what it was. But a complete criticism does not end there. In the evolution of abstract doctrine as we find it written in the history of philosophy, if there is always, on one side, the fatal, irresistible, mechanic play of circumstance—the circumstances of a particular age, which may be analysed and explained; there is always also, as if acting from the opposite side, the comparatively inexplicable force of a personality, resistant to, while it is moulded by, them. It might even be said that the trial-task of criticism, in regard to literature and art no less than to philosophy, begins exactly where the estimate of general conditions, of the conditions common to all the products of this or that particular age—of the 'environment'—leaves off, and we touch what is unique in the individual genius which contrived after all, by force of will, to have its own masterful way with that environment. If in reading Plato, for instance, the philosophic student has to reconstruct for himself, as far as possible, the general character of an *age*, he must also, so far as he may, reproduce the portrait of a *person*. The Sophists, the Sophistical world, around him; his master, Socrates; the Pre-Socratic philosophies; the mechanic influence, that is to say, of past and present:—of course we can know nothing at all of the Platonic doctrine except so far as we see it in well-ascertained contact with all that; but there is also Plato himself in it.

Literary Criticism

JOACHIM DU BELLAY[1]

In the middle of the sixteenth century, when the spirit of the Renaissance was everywhere, and people had begun to look back with distaste on the works of the middle age, the old Gothic manner had still one chance more, in borrowing something from the rival which was about to supplant it. In this way there was produced, chiefly in France, a new and peculiar phase of taste with qualities and a charm of its own, blending the somewhat attenuated grace of Italian ornament with the general outlines of Northern design. It created the *Château de Gaillon*, as you may still see it in the delicate engravings of Israël Silvestre—a Gothic donjon veiled faintly by a surface of dainty Italian traceries—Chenonceaux, Blois, Chambord, and the church of Brou. In painting, there came from Italy workmen like *Maître Roux* and the masters of the school of Fontainebleau, to have their later Italian voluptuousness attempered by the naïve and silvery qualities of the native style; and it was characteristic of these painters that they were most successful in painting on glass, an art so essentially medieval. Taking it up where the middle age had left it, they found their whole work among the last subtleties of colour and line; and keeping within the true limits of their material, they got quite a new order of effects from it, and felt their way to refinements on colour never dreamed of by those older workmen, the glass-painters of Chartres or Le Mans. What is called the *Renaissance in France* is thus not so much the introduction of a wholly new taste ready-made from Italy, but rather the finest and subtlest phase of the middle age itself, its last fleeting splendour and temperate Saint Martin's summer. In poetry, the Gothic spirit in France had produced a thousand songs; so in the Renaissance, French poetry too did but borrow something to blend with a native growth, and the poems of Ronsard, with their ingenuity, their delicately figured surfaces, their slightness, their fanciful combinations of rhyme, are the correlative of the traceries of the house of Jacques Cœur at Bourges, or the *Maison de Justice* at Rouen.[2]

There was indeed something in the native French taste naturally akin to that Italian *finesse*. The characteristic of French work had always been a certain nicety, a remarkable daintiness of hand, *une netteté remarquable d'exécution*. In the paintings of François Clouet, for example, or rather of the Clouets—for there was a whole family of them—painters remarkable for their resistance to Italian influences, there is a silveriness of colour and a clearness of expression which distinguish them very definitely from their Flemish neighbours, Hemling or the Van Eycks. And this nicety is not less characteristic of old French poetry. A light, aërial delicacy, a simple elegance—*une netteté remarquable d'exécution*: these are essential characteristics alike of Villon's poetry, and of the *Hours of Anne of Brittany*. They are characteristic too of a hundred French Gothic carvings and traceries. Alike in the old Gothic cathedrals, and in their counterpart, the old Gothic *chansons de geste*, the rough and ponderous mass becomes, as if by passing for a moment into happier conditions, or through a more gracious stratum of air, graceful and refined, like the carved ferneries on the granite church at Folgoat, or the lines which describe the fair priestly hands of Archbishop Turpin, in the song of Roland ; although below both alike there is a fund of mere Gothic strength, or heaviness.*

Now Villon's songs and Clouet's painting are like these. It is the higher touch making itself felt here and there, betraying itself, like nobler blood in a lower stock, by a fine line or gesture or expression, the turn of a wrist, the tapering of a finger. In Ronsard's time that rougher element seemed likely to predominate. No one can turn over the pages of Rabelais without feeling how much need there was of softening, of castigation. To effect this softening is the object of the revolution in poetry which is connected with Ronsard's name.[3] Casting about for the means of thus refining upon and saving the character of French literature, he accepted that influx of Renaissance taste, which, leaving the buildings, the language, the art, the poetry of France, at bottom, what they were, old French Gothic still, gilds their surfaces with a strange, delightful, foreign aspect passing over all that Northern land, in itself neither deeper nor more permanent than a chance effect of light. He reinforces, he doubles the French daintiness by Italian *finesse*. Thereupon, nearly all the force and all the seriousness of French work disappear ; only the elegance, the aërial touch, the perfect manner remain. But this elegance, this manner, this daintiness of execution are consummate, and have an unmistakable æsthetic value.

So the old French *chanson*, which, like the old northern Gothic ornament, though it sometimes refined itself into a sort of weird elegance, was often, in its essence, something rude and formless,

* The purely artistic aspects of this subject have been interpreted, in a work of great taste and learning, by Mrs Mark Pattison:—*The Renaissance of Art in France*.

became in the hands of Ronsard a Pindaric ode. He gave it structure, a sustained system, *strophe* and *antistrophe*, and taught it a changefulness and variety of metre which keep the curiosity always excited, so that the very aspect of it, as it lies written on the page, carries the eye lightly onwards, and of which this is a good instance :—

> *Avril, la grace, et le ris*
> > *De Cypris,*
> *Le flair et la douce haleine;*
> *Avril, le parfum des dieux,*
> > *Qui, des cieux,*
> *Sentent l'odeur de la plaine;*
>
> *C'est toy, courtois et gentil,*
> > *Qui, d'exil*
> *Retire ces passageres,*
> *Ces arondelles qui vont,*
> > *Et qui sont*
> *Du printemps les messageres.*

That is not by Ronsard, but by Remy Belleau, for Ronsard soon came to have a school. Six other poets threw in their lot with him in his literary revolution,—this Remy Belleau, Antoine de Baif, Pontus de Tyard, Étienne Jodelle, Jean Daurat, and lastly Joachim du Bellay; and with that strange love of emblems which is characteristic of the time, which covered all the works of Francis the First with the salamander, and all the works of Henry the Second with the double crescent, and all the works of Anne of Brittany with the knotted cord, they called themselves the *Pleiad*; seven in all, although, as happens with the celestial Pleiad, if you scrutinise this constellation of poets more carefully you may find there a great number of minor stars.

The first note of this literary revolution was struck by Joachim du Bellay in a little tract written at the early age of twenty-four, which coming to us through three centuries seems of yesterday, so full is it of those delicate critical distinctions which are sometimes supposed peculiar to modern writers. The piece has for its title *La Deffense et Illustration de la langue Françoyse*; and its problem is how to illustrate or ennoble the French language, to give it lustre. We are accustomed to speak of the varied critical and creative movement of the fifteenth and sixteenth centuries as the *Renaissance*, and because we have a single name for it we may sometimes fancy that there was more unity in the thing itself than there really was. Even the Reformation, that other great movement of the fifteenth and sixteenth centuries, had far less unity, far less of combined action, than is at first sight supposed; and the Renaissance was infinitely less united, less conscious of combined action, than the Reformation. But if anywhere the Renaissance became conscious, as a German philosopher [4] might say, if ever it was understood as a systematic movement by those who took part in it, it is in this little book of Joachim du Bellay's which it is impossible to read without feeling the excitement, the animation, of change, of discovery. 'It is a remarkable fact', says M. Sainte-Beuve, 'and an inversion of what is true of other languages, that, in French, prose has always had the precedence over poetry.' Du Bellay's prose is perfectly transparent, flexible, and chaste. In many ways it is a more characteristic example of the culture of the *Pleiad* than any of its verse; and those who love the whole movement of which the *Pleiad* is a part, for a weird foreign grace in it, and may be looking about for a true specimen of it, cannot have a better than Joachim du Bellay and this little treatise of his.

Du Bellay's object is to adjust the existing French culture to the rediscovered classical culture; and in discussing this problem, and developing the theories of the *Pleiad*, he has lighted upon many principles of permanent truth and applicability. There were some who despaired of the French language altogether, who thought it naturally incapable of the fulness and elegance of Greek and Latin—*cette élégance et copie qui est en la langue Greque et Romaine*—that science could be adequately discussed, and poetry nobly written, only in the dead languages. 'Those who speak thus', says Du Bellay, 'make me think of the relics which one may only see through a little pane of glass, and must not touch with one's hands. That is what these people do with all branches of culture, which they keep shut up in Greek and Latin books, not permitting one to see them otherwise, or transport them out of dead words into those which are alive, and wing their way daily through the mouths of men.' 'Languages', he says again, 'are not born like plants and trees, some naturally feeble and sickly, others healthy and strong and apter to bear the weight of men's conceptions, but all their virtue is generated in the world of choice and men's freewill concerning them. Therefore, I cannot blame too strongly the rashness of some of our countrymen, who being anything rather than Greeks or Latins, depreciate and reject with more than stoical disdain everything written in French; nor can I express my surprise at the odd opinion of some learned men who think that our vulgar tongue is wholly incapable of erudition and good literature.'

It was an age of translations. Du Bellay himself translated two books of the *Æneid*, and other poetry, old and new, and there were some who thought that the translation of the classical literature was the true means of *ennobling* the French language:—strangers are ever favourites with us—*nous favorisons toujours les étrangers*. Du Bellay moderates their expectations. 'I do not believe that one can learn the right use of them'—he is speaking of figures and ornament in language—'from translations, because it is impossible to reproduce them with the same grace with which the original author used them. For each language has I know not what peculiarity of its own; and if you force yourself to express the naturalness (*le naïf*) of this in another language, observing the law of translation,—not to expatiate beyond the limits of the author himself, your words will be constrained, cold and ungraceful.' Then he fixes the test of all good translation:—'To prove this, read me Demosthenes and Homer in Latin, Cicero and Virgil in French, and see whether they produce in you the same affections which you experience in reading those authors in the original.'

In this effort to ennoble the French language, to give it grace, number, perfection, and as painters do to their pictures, that last, so desirable, touch—*cette dernière main que nous désirons*—what Du Bellay is really pleading for is his mother-tongue, the language, that is, in which one will have the utmost degree of what is moving and passionate. He recognised of what force the music and dignity of languages are, how they enter into the inmost part of things; and in pleading for the cultivation of the French language, he is pleading for no merely scholastic interest, but for freedom, impulse, reality, not in literature only, but in daily communion of speech. After all, it was impossible to have this impulse in Greek and Latin, dead languages shut up in books as in reliquaries—*péris et mises en reliquaires de livres*. By aid of this starveling stock—*pauvre plante et vergette*—of the French language, he must speak delicately, movingly, if he is ever to speak so at all: that, or none, must be for him the medium of what he calls, in one of his great phrases, *le discours fatal des choses mondaines*—that discourse about affairs which decides men's fates. And it is his patriotism not to despair of it; he sees it already perfect in all elegance and beauty of words—*parfait en toute élégance et vénusté de paroles*.

Du Bellay was born in the disastrous year 1525, the year of the battle of Pavia, and the captivity of Francis the First. His parents died early, and to him, as the younger son, his mother's little estate, *ce petit Liré*, the beloved place of his birth, descended. He was brought up by a brother only a little older than himself; and left to themselves, the two boys passed their lives in day-dreams of military glory. Their education was neglected; 'The time of my youth', says Du Bellay, 'was lost, like the flower which no shower waters, and no hand cultivates'. He was just twenty years old when the elder brother died, leaving Joachim to be the guardian of his child. It was with regret, with a shrinking sense of incapacity, that he took upon him the burden of this responsibility. Hitherto he had looked forward to the profession of a soldier, hereditary in his family. But at this time a sickness attacked him which brought him cruel sufferings, and seemed likely to be mortal. It was then for the first time that he read the Greek and Latin poets. These studies came too late to make him what he so much desired to be, a trifler in Greek and Latin verse, like so many others of his time now forgotten; instead, they made him a lover of his own homely native tongue, that poor starveling stock of the French language. It was through this fortunate short-coming in his education that he became national and modern; and he learned afterwards to look back on that wild garden of his youth with only a half regret. A certain Cardinal du Bellay was the successful member of the family, a man often employed in high official business. To him the thoughts of Joachim turned when it became necessary to choose a profession, and in 1552 he accompanied the Cardinal to Rome. He remained there nearly five years, burdened with the weight of affairs, and languishing with home-sickness.[5] Yet it was under these circumstances that his genius yielded its best fruits. From Rome, so full of pleasurable sensation for men of an imaginative temperament such as his, with all the curiosities of the Renaissance still fresh in it, his thoughts went back painfully, longingly, to the country of the Loire, with its wide expanse of waving corn, its homely pointed roofs of grey slate, and its far-off scent of the sea. He reached home at last, but only to die there, quite suddenly, one wintry day, at the early age of thirty-five.

Much of Du Bellay's poetry illustrates rather the age and school to which he belonged than his own temper and genius. As with the writings of Ronsard and the other poets of the *Pleiad*, its interest depends not so much on the impress of individual genius upon it, as on the circumstance that it was once poetry *à la mode*, that it is part of the manner of a time—a time which made much of manner, and carried it to a high degree of perfection. It is one of the decorations of an age which threw a large part of its energy into the work of decoration. We feel a pensive pleasure in gazing on these faded adornments, and observing how a group of actual men and women pleased themselves long ago. Ronsard's poems are a kind of epitome of his age. Of one side of that age, it is true, of the strenuous, the progressive, the serious movement, which was then going on, there is little; but of the catholic side, the losing side, the forlorn hope, hardly a figure is absent. The Queen of Scots, at whose desire Ronsard published his

odes, reading him in her northern prison, felt that he was bringing
back to her the true flavour of her early days in the court of Catherine
at the Louvre, with its exotic Italian gaieties. Those who disliked that
poetry, disliked it because they found that age itself distasteful. The
poetry of Malherbe came, with its sustained style and weighty sentiment, but with nothing that set people singing; and the lovers of
such poetry saw in the poetry of the *Pleiad* only the latest trumpery
of the middle age. But the time arrived when the school of Malherbe
also had had its day; and the *Romanticists*, who in their eagerness for
excitement, for strange music and imagery, went back to the works
of the middle age, accepted the *Pleiad* too with the rest; and in that
new middle age which their genius has evoked, the poetry of the
Pleiad has found its place.[6] At first, with Malherbe, you may think it,
like the architecture, the whole mode of life, the very dresses of that
time, fantastic, faded, *rococo*. But if you look long enough to understand it, to conceive its sentiment, you will find that those wanton
lines have a spirit guiding their caprices. For there is *style* there; one
temper has shaped the whole; and everything that has style, that has
been done as no other man or age could have done it, as it could
never, for all our trying, be done again, has its true value and interest.
Let us dwell upon it for a moment, and try to gather from it that
special flower, *ce fleur particulier*, which Ronsard himself tells us every
garden has.

It is poetry not for the people, but for a confined circle, for courtiers,
great lords and erudite persons, people who desire to be humoured,
to gratify a certain refined voluptousness they have in them. Ronsard
loves, or dreams that he loves, a rare and peculiar type of beauty, *la
petite pucelle Angevine*, with golden hair and dark eyes. But he has the
ambition not only of being a courtier and a lover, but a great scholar
also; he is anxious about orthography, about the letter *è Grecque*, the
true spelling of Latin names in French writing, and the restoration of
the letter *i* to its primitive liberty—*del' i voyelle en sa première liberté*.
His poetry is full of quaint, remote learning. He is just a little pedantic,
true always to his own express judgment, that to be natural is not
enough for one who in poetry desires to produce work worthy of
immortality. And therewithal a certain number of Greek words,
which charmed Ronsard and his circle by their gaiety and daintiness,
and a certain air of foreign elegance about them, crept into the
French language; as there were other strange words which the poets
of the *Pleiad* forged for themselves, and which had only an ephemeral
existence.

With this was united the desire to taste a more exquisite and various
music than that of the older French verse, or of the classical poets. The

music of the measured, scanned verse of Latin and Greek poetry is one thing; the music of the rhymed, unscanned verse of Villon and the old French poets, *la poésie chantée*, is another. To combine these two kinds of music in a new school of French poetry, to make verse which should scan and rhyme as well, to search out and harmonise the measure of every syllable, and unite it to the swift, flitting, swallow-like motion of rhyme, to penetrate their poetry with a double music —this was the ambition of the *Pleiad*. They are insatiable of music, they cannot have enough of it; they desire a music of greater compass perhaps than words can possibly yield, to drain out the last drops of sweetness which a certain note or accent contains.

It was Goudimel, the serious and protestant Goudimel, who set Ronsard's songs to music; but except in this eagerness for music the poets of the *Pleiad* seem never quite in earnest. The old Greek and Roman mythology, which the great Italians had found a motive so weighty and severe, becomes with them a mere toy. That 'Lord of terrible aspect', *Amor*, has become Love the boy, or the babe. They are full of fine railleries; they delight in diminutives, *ondelette, fontelette, doucelette, Cassandrette*. Their loves are only half real, a vain effort to prolong the imaginative loves of the middle age beyond their natural lifetime. They write love-poems for hire. Like that party of people who tell the tales in Boccaccio's *Decameron*, they form a circle which in an age of great troubles, losses, anxieties, can amuse itself with art, poetry, intrigue. But they amuse themselves with wonderful elegance. And sometimes their gaiety becomes satiric, for, as they play, real passions insinuate themselves, and at least the reality of death. Their dejection at the thought of leaving this fair abode of our common day-light—*le beau séjour du commun jour*—is expressed by them with almost wearisome reiteration. But with this sentiment too they are able to trifle. The imagery of death serves for delicate ornament, and they weave into the airy nothingness of their verses their trite reflections on the vanity of life. Just so the grotesque details of the charnel-house nest themselves, together with birds and flowers and the fancies of the pagan mythology, in the traceries of the architecture of that time, which wantons in its graceful arabesques, with the images of old age and death.

Ronsard became deaf at sixteen; and it was this circumstance which finally determined him to be a man of letters instead of a diplomatist, significantly, one might fancy, of a certain premature agedness, and of the tranquil, temperate sweetness appropriate to that, in the school of poetry which he founded. Its charm is that of a thing not vigorous or original, but full of the grace which comes of long study and reiterated refinements, and many steps repeated, and many angles worn down, with an exquisite faintness, *une fadeur exquise*, a certain tenuity and caducity, as for those who can bear nothing vehement or strong; for princes weary of love, like Francis the First, or of pleasure, like Henry the Third, or of action, like Henry the Fourth. Its merits are those of the old,—grace and finish, perfect in minute detail. For these people are a little jaded, and have a constant desire for a subdued and delicate excitement, to warm their creeping fancy a little. They love a constant change of rhyme in poetry, and in their houses that strange, fantastic interweaving of thin, reed-like lines, which are a kind of rhetoric in architecture.

But the poetry of the *Pleiad* is true not only to the physiognomy of its age, but also to its country—*ce pays du Vendomois*—the names and scenery of which so often recur in it:—the great Loire, with its long spaces of white sand; the little river Loir; the heathy, upland country, with its scattered pools of water and waste roadsides, and retired manors, with their crazy old feudal defences half fallen into decay; *La Beauce*, where the vast rolling fields seem to anticipate the great western sea itself. It is full of the traits of that country. We see Du Bellay and Ronsard gardening, or hunting with their dogs, or watch the pastimes of a rainy day; and with all this is connected a domesticity, a homeliness and simple goodness, by which the Northern country gains upon the South. They have the love of the aged for warmth, and understand the poetry of winter; for they are not far from the Atlantic, and the west wind which comes up from it, turning the poplars white, spares not this new Italy in France. So the fireside often appears, with the pleasures of the frosty season, about the vast emblazoned chimneys of the time, and with a *bonhomie* as of little children, or old people.

It is in Du Bellay's *Olive*, a collection of sonnets in praise of a half-imaginary lady, *Sonnetz a la louange d'Olive*, that these characteristics are most abundant. Here is a perfectly crystallised example:—

> *D'amour, de grace, et de haulte valeur*
> *Les feux divins estoient ceinctz et les cieulx*
> *S'estoient vestuz d'un manteau precieux*
> *A raiz ardens de diverse couleur:*
> *Tout estoit plein de beauté, de bonheur,*
> *La mer tranquille, et le vent gracieulx,*
> *Quand celle la nasquit en ces bas lieux*
> *Qui a pillé du monde tout l'honneur.*
> *Ell' prist son teint des beux lyz blanchissans,*
> *Son chef de l'or, ses deux levres des rozes,*
> *Et du soleil ses yeux resplandissans:*

Le ciel usant de liberalité.
Mist en l'esprit ses semences encloses,
Son nom des Dieux prist l'immortalité.

That he is thus a characteristic specimen of the poetical taste of
that age, is indeed Du Bellay's chief interest. But if his work is to have
the highest sort of interest, if it is to do something more than satisfy
curiosity, if it is to have an æsthetic as distinct from an historical
value, it is not enough for a poet to have been the true child of his
age, to have conformed to its æsthetic conditions, and by so conforming to have charmed and stimulated that age; it is necessary that
there should be perceptible in his work something individual,
inventive, unique, the impress there of the writer's own temper and
personality. This impress M. Sainte-Beuve thought he found in the
Antiquités de Rome, and the *Regrets*, which he ranks as what has been
called *poésie intime*, that intensely modern sort of poetry in which the
writer has for his aim the portraiture of his own most intimate moods,
and to take the reader into his confidence. That age had other instances of this intimacy of sentiment: Montaigne's *Essays* are full of it,
the carvings of the church of Brou are full of it. M. Sainte-Beuve has
perhaps exaggerated the influence of this quality in Du Bellay's
Regrets; but the very name of the book has a touch of Rousseau about
it, and reminds one of a whole generation of self-pitying poets in
modern times. It was in the atmosphere of Rome, to him so strange
and mournful, that these pale flowers grew up. For that journey to
Italy, which he deplored as the greatest misfortune of his life, put him
in full possession of his talent, and brought out all its originality. And
in effect you do find intimacy, *intimité*, here. The trouble of his life is
analysed, and the sentiment of it conveyed directly to our minds;
not a great sorrow or passion, but only the sense of loss in passing days,
the *ennui* of a dreamer who must plunge into the world's affairs, the
opposition between actual life and the ideal, a longing for rest,
nostalgia, home-sickness—that pre-eminently childish, but so suggestive sorrow, as significant of the final regeret of all human creatures
for the familiar earth and limited sky.

The feeling for landscape is often described as a modern one; still
more so is that for antiquity, the sentiment of ruins. Du Bellay has
this sentiment. The duration of the hard, sharp outlines of things is a
grief to him, and passing his wearisome days among the ruins of
ancient Rome, he is consoled by the thought that all must one day
end, by the sentiment of the grandeur of nothingness—*la grandeur du
rien*. With a strange touch of far-off mysticism, he thinks that the great
whole—*le grand tout*—into which all other things pass and lose them-

selves, ought itself sometimes to perish and pass away. Nothing less can relieve his weariness. From the stately aspects of Rome his thoughts went back continually to France, to the smoking chimneys of his little village, the longer twilight of the North, the soft climate of Anjou— *la douceur Angevine*; yet not so much to the real France, we may be sure, with its dark streets and roofs of rough-hewn slate, as to that other country, with slenderer towers, and more winding rivers, and trees like flowers, and with softer sunshine on more gracefully-proportioned fields and ways, which the fancy of the exile, and the pilgrim, and of the schoolboy far from home, and of those kept at home unwillingly, everywhere builds up before or behind them.

He came home at last, through the *Grisons*, by slow journeys; and there, in the cooler air of his own country, under its skies of milkier blue, the sweetest flower of his genius sprang up. There have been poets whose whole fame has rested on one poem, as Gray's on the *Elegy in a Country Churchyard*, or Ronsard's, as many critics have thought, on the eighteen lines of one famous ode. Du Bellay has almost been the poet of one poem; and this one poem of his is an Italian product transplanted into that green country of Anjou; out of the Latin verses of Andrea Navagero, into French. But it is a composition in which the matter is almost nothing, and the form almost everything; and the form of the poem as it stands, written in old French, is all Du Bellay's own. It is a song which the winnowers are supposed to sing as they winnow the corn, and they invoke the winds to lie lightly on the grain.

D'UN VANNEUR DE BLE AUX VENTS.*

> A vous trouppe legère
>   Qui d'aile passagère
>   Par le monde volez,
>   Et d'un sifflant murmure
>   L'ombrageuse verdure
>   Doulcement esbranlez.
>
> J'offre ces violettes,
>   Ces lis & ces fleurettes,
>   Et ces roses icy,
>   Ces vermeillettes roses
>   Sont freschement écloses,
>   Et ces œlliets aussi.

* A graceful translation of this and some other poems of the *Pleiad* may be found in *Ballads and Lyrics of Old France*, by Mr Andrew Lang.[7]

> *De vostre doulce haleine*
> *Eventez ceste plaine*
> *Eventez ce sejour;*
> *Ce pendant que j'ahanne*
> *A mon blè que je vanne*
> *A la chaleur du jour.*

That has, in the highest degree, the qualities, the value, of the whole Pleiad school of poetry, of the whole phase of taste from which that school derives—a certain silvery grace of fancy, nearly all the pleasure of which is in the surprise at the happy and dexterous way in which a thing slight in itself is handled. The sweetness of it is by no means to be got at by crushing, as you crush wild herbs to get at their perfume. One seems to hear the measured motion of the fans, with a child's pleasure on coming across the incident for the first time, in one of those great barns of Du Bellay's own country, *La Beauce*, the granary of France. A sudden light transfigures some trivial thing, a weather-vane, a windmill, a winnowing fan, the dust in the barn door. A moment—and the thing has vanished, because it was pure effect; but it leaves a relish behind it, a longing that the accident may happen again.

ÆSTHETIC POETRY[1]

The 'æsthetic' poetry is neither a mere reproduction of Greek or medieval poetry, nor only an idealisation of modern life and sentiment. The atmosphere on which its effect depends belongs to no simple form of poetry, no actual form of life. Greek poetry, medieval or modern poetry, projects, above the realities of its time, a world in which the forms of things are transfigured. Of that transfigured world this new poetry takes possession, and sublimates beyond it another still fainter and more spectral, which is literally an artificial or 'earthly paradise'. It is a finer ideal, extracted from what in relation to any actual world is already an ideal. Like some strange second flowering after date, it renews on a more delicate type the poetry of a past age, but must not be confounded with it. The secret of the enjoyment of it is that inversion of home-sickness known to some, that incurable thirst for the sense of escape, which no actual form of life satisfies, no poetry even, if it be merely simple and spontaneous.

The writings of the 'romantic school', of which the æsthetic poetry is an afterthought, mark a transition not so much from the pagan to the medieval ideal, as from a lower to a higher degree of passion in literature. The end of the eighteenth century, swept by vast disturbing currents, experienced an excitement of spirit of which one note was a reaction against an outworn classicism severed not more from nature than from the genuine motives of ancient art; and a return to true Hellenism was as much a part of this reaction as the sudden preoccupation with things medieval. The medieval tendency is in Goethe's *Goetz von Berlichingen*, the Hellenic in his *Iphigenie*. At first this medievalism was superficial, or at least external. Adventure, romance in the frankest sense, grotesque individualism—that is one element in medieval poetry, and with it alone Scott and Goethe dealt. Beyond them were the two other elements of the medieval spirit: its mystic religion at its apex in Dante and Saint Louis, and its mystic passion, passing here and there into the great romantic loves of rebellious flesh, of Lancelot and Abelard. That stricter, imaginative medievalism which re-creates the mind of the

95

Middle Age, so that the form, the presentment grows outward from within, came later with Victor Hugo in France, with Heine in Germany.

In the *Defence of Guenevere: and Other Poems*, published by Mr William Morris now many years ago, the first typical specimen of æsthetic poetry, we have a refinement upon this later, profounder medievalism. The poem which gives its name to the volume is a thing tormented and awry with passion, like the body of Guenevere defending herself from the charge of adultery, and the accent falls in strange, unwonted places with the effect of a great cry. In truth these Arthurian legends, in their origin prior to Christianity, yield all their sweetness only in a Christian atmosphere. What is characteristic in them is the strange suggestion of a deliberate choice between Christ and a rival lover.[2] That religion, monastic religion at any rate, has its sensuous side, a dangerously sensuous side, has been often seen: it is the experience of Rousseau as well as of the Christian mystics. The Christianity of the Middle Age made way among a people whose loss was in the life of the senses partly by its æsthetic beauty, a thing so profoundly felt by the Latin hymn-writers, who for one moral or spiritual sentiment have a hundred sensuous images. And so in those imaginative loves, in their highest expression, the Provençal poetry, it is a rival religion with a new rival *cultus* that we see. Coloured through and through with Christian sentiment, they are rebels against it. The rejection of one worship for another is never lost sight of. The jealousy of that other lover, for whom these words and images and refined ways of sentiment were first devised, is the secret here of a borrowed, perhaps factitious colour and heat. It is the mood of the cloister taking a new direction, and winning so a later space of life it never anticipated.

Hereon, as before in the cloister, so now in the *château*, the reign of reverie set in. The devotion of the cloister knew that mood thoroughly, and had sounded all its stops. For the object of this devotion was absent or veiled, not limited to one supreme plastic form like Zeus at Olympia or Athena in the Acropolis, but distracted, as in a fever dream, into a thousand symbols and reflections.[3] But then, the Church, that new Sibyl, had a thousand secrets to make the absent near. Into this kingdom of reverie, and with it into a paradise of ambitious refinements, the earthly love enters, and becomes a prolonged somnambulism. Of religion it learns the art of directing towards an unseen object sentiments whose natural direction is towards objects of sense. Hence a love defined by the absence of the beloved, choosing to be without hope, protesting against all lower uses of love, barren, extravagant, antinomian. It is the love which is incompatible with marriage, for the chevalier who never comes, of the serf for the *châtelaine*, of the rose for the nightingale, of Rudel for the Lady of Tripoli. Another element of extravagance came in with the feudal spirit: Provençal love is full of the very forms of vassalage. To be the servant of love, to have offended, to taste the subtle luxury of chastisement, of reconciliation—the religious spirit, too, knows that, and meets just there, as in Rousseau, the delicacies of the earthly love. Here, under this strange complex of conditions, as in some medicated air, exotic flowers of sentiment expand, among people of a remote and unaccustomed beauty, somnambulistic, frail, androgynous, the light almost shining through them. Surely, such loves were too fragile and adventurous to last more than for a moment.

That monastic religion of the Middle Age was, in fact, in many of its bearings, like a beautiful disease or disorder of the senses: and a religion which is a disorder of the senses must always be subject to illusions. Reverie, illusion, delirium: they are the three stages of a fatal descent both in the religion and the loves of the Middle Age. Nowhere has the impression of this delirium been conveyed as by Victor Hugo in *Notre Dame de Paris*. The strangest creations of sleep seem here, by some appalling licence, to cross the limit of the dawn. The English poet too has learned the secret. He has diffused through *King Arthur's Tomb* the maddening white glare of the sun, and tyranny of the moon, not tender and far-off, but close down—the sorcerer's moon, large and feverish. The colouring is intricate and delirious, as of 'scarlet lilies'. The influence of summer is like a poison in one's blood, with a sudden bewildered sickening of life and all things. In *Galahad: a Mystery*, the frost of Christmas night on the chapel stones acts as a strong narcotic: a sudden shrill rinigng pierces through the numbness: a voice proclaims that the Grail has gone forth through the great forest. It is in the *Blue Closet* that this delirium reaches its height with a singular beauty, reserved perhaps for the enjoyment of the few.

A passion of which the outlets are sealed, begets a tension of nerve, in which the sensible world comes to one with a reinforced brilliancy and relief—all redness is turned into blood, all waters into tears. Hence a wild, convulsed sensuousness in the poetry of the Middle Age, in which the things of nature begin to play a strange delirious part. Of the things of nature the medieval mind had a deep sense; but its sense of them was not objective, no real escape to the world without us. The aspects and motions of nature only reinforced its prevailing mood, and were in conspiracy with one's own brain against one. A single sentiment invaded the world: everything was infused with a motive drawn from the soul. The amorous poetry of Provence, making the starling and the swallow its messengers, illustrates the whole attitude of nature in this electric atmosphere, bent as by miracle or magic to the service of human passion.

The most popular and gracious form of Provençal poetry was the *nocturn,* sung by the lover at night at the door or under the window of his mistress. These songs were of different kinds, according to the hour at which they were intended to be sung. Some were to be sung at midnight—songs inviting to sleep, the *serena,* or *serenade*; others at break of day—waking songs, the *aube,* or *aubade.** This waking-song is put sometimes into the mouth of a comrade of the lover, who plays sentinel during the night, to watch for and announce the dawn: sometimes into the mouth of one of the lovers, who are about to separate. A modification of it is familiar to us all in *Romeo and Juliet,* where the lovers debate whether the song they hear is of the nightingale or the lark; the aubade, with the two other great forms of love-poetry then floating in the world, the sonnet and the epithalamium, being here refined, heightened, and inwoven into the structure of the play. Those, in whom what Rousseau calls *les frayeurs nocturnes* are constitutional, know what splendour they give to the things of the morning; and how there comes something of relief from physical pain with the first white film in the sky. The Middle Age knew those terrors in all their forms; and these songs of the morning win hence a strange tenderness and effect. The crown of the English poet's book is one of these appreciations of the dawn:—

> 'Pray but one prayer for me 'twixt thy closed lips,
>   Think but one thought of me up in the stars.
> The summer-night waneth, the morning light slips,
>   Faint and gray 'twixt the leaves of the aspen,
>   betwixt the cloud-bars,
> That are patiently waiting there for the dawn:
>   Patient and colourless, though Heaven's gold
> Waits to float through them along with the sun.
> Far out in the meadows, above the young corn,
>   The heavy elms wait, and restless and cold
> The uneasy wind rises; the roses are dun;
> Through the long twilight they pray for the dawn,
> Round the lone house in the midst of the corn.
>   Speak but one word to me over the corn,
>   Over the tender, bow'd locks of the corn.'

---

* Fauriel's *Histoire de la Poésie Provençale,* tome ii. ch. xviii.

It is the very soul of the bridegroom which goes forth to the bride: inanimate things are longing with him: all the sweetness of the imaginative loves of the Middle Age, with a superadded spirituality of touch all its own, is in that!

The *Defence of Guenevere* was published in 1858; the *Life and Death of Jason* in 1867; to be followed by *The Earthly Paradise*; and the change of manner wrought in the interval, entire, almost a revolt, is characteristic of the æsthetic poetry. Here there is no delirium or illusion, no experiences of mere soul while the body and the bodily senses sleep, or wake with convulsed intensity at the prompting of imaginative love; but rather the great primary passions under broad daylight as of the pagan Veronese. This simplification interests us, not merely for the sake of an individual poet—full of charm as he is—but chiefly because it explains through him a transition which, under many forms, is one law of the life of the human spirit, and of which what we call the Renaissance is only a supreme instance. Just so the monk in his cloister, through the 'open vision', open only to the spirit, divined, aspired to, and at last apprehended, a better daylight, but earthly, open only to the senses. Complex and subtle interests, which the mind spins for itself may occupy art and poetry or our own spirits for a time; but sooner or later they come back with a sharp rebound to the simple elementary passions—anger, desire, regret, pity, and fear; and what corresponds to them in the sensuous world—bare, abstract, fire, water, air, tears, sleep, silence, and what De Quincey has called the 'glory of motion'.

This reaction from dreamlight to daylight gives, as always happens, a strange power in dealing with morning and the things of the morning. Not less in this Hellenist of the Middle Age master of dreams, of sleep and the desire of sleep—sleep in which no one walks, restorer of childhood to men—dreams, not like Galahad's or Guenevere's, but full of happy, childish wonder as in the earlier world. It is a world in which the centaur and the ram with the fleece of gold are conceivable. The song sung always claims to be sung for the first time. There are hints at a language common to birds and beasts and men. Everywhere there is an impression of surprise, as of people first waking from the golden age, at fire, snow, wine, the touch of water as one swims, the salt taste of the sea. And this simplicity at first hand is a strange contrast to the sought-out simplicity of Wordsworth. Desire here is towards the body of nature for its own sake, not because a soul is divined through it.

And yet it is one of the charming anachronisms of a poet, who, while he handles an ancient subject, never becomes an antiquarian, but animates his subject by keeping it always close to himself, that betweenwhiles we have a sense of English scenery as from an eye well practised under Wordsworth's influence, as from 'the casement half opened on summer-nights', with the song of the brown bird among the willows, the

> 'Noise of bells, such as in moonlit lanes
> Rings from the grey team on the market night.'

Nowhere but in England is there such a 'paradise of birds', the fern-owl, the water-hen, the thrush in a hundred sweet variations, the ger-falcon, the kestrel, the starling, the pea-fowl; birds heard from the field by the townsman down in the streets at dawn; doves every-where, pink-footed, grey-winged, flitting about the temple, troubled by the temple incense, trapped in the snow. The sea-touches are not less sharp and firm, surest of effect in places where river and sea, salt and fresh waves, conflict.

In handling a subject of Greek legend, anything in the way of an actual revival must always be impossible. Such vain antiquarianism is a waste of the poet's power. The composite experience of all the ages is part of each one of us: to deduct from that experience, to obliterate any part of it, to come face to face with the people of a past age, as if the Middle Age, the Renaissance, the eighteenth century had not been, is as impossible as to become a little child, or enter again into the womb and be born. But though it is not possible to repress a single phase of that humanity, which, because we live and move and have our being in the life of humanity, makes us what we are, it is possible to isolate such a phase, to throw it into relief, to be divided against ourselves in zeal for it; as we may hark back to some choice space of our own individual life. We cannot truly conceive the age: we can conceive the element it has contributed to our culture: we can treat the subjects of the age bringing that into relief. Such an attitude towards Greece, aspiring to but never actually reaching its way of conceiving life, is what is possible for art.

The modern poet or artist who treats in this way a classical story comes very near, if not to the Hellenism of Homer, yet to the Hellen-ism of Chaucer, the Hellenism of the Middle Age, or rather of that exquisite first period of the Renaissance within it. Afterwards the Renaissance takes its side, becomes, perhaps, exaggerated or facile. But the choice life of the human spirit is always under mixed lights, and in mixed situations, when it is not too sure of itself, is still expec-tant, girt up to leap forward to the promise. Such a situation there was in that earliest return from the overwrought spiritualities of the Middle Age to the earlier, more ancient life of the senses; and for us the most attractive form of classical story is the monk's conception of it, when he escapes from the sombre atmosphere of his cloister to natural light. The fruits of this mood, which, divining more than it understands, infuses into the scenery and figures of Christian history some subtle reminiscence of older gods, or into the story of Cupid and Psyche that passionate stress of spirit which the world owes to Christianity, constitute a peculiar vein of interest in the art of the fifteenth century.

And so, before we leave *Jason* and *The Earthly Paradise*, a word must be said about their medievalisms, delicate inconsistencies, which, coming in a poem of Greek subject, bring into this white dawn thoughts of the delirious night just over and make one's sense of relief deeper. The opening of the fourth book of *Jason* describes the embarkation of the Argonauts: as in a dream, the scene shifts and we go down from Iolchos to the sea through a pageant of the Middle Age in some French or Italian town. The gilded vanes on the spires, the bells ringing in the towers, the trellis of roses at the window, the close planted with apple-trees, the grotesque undercroft with its close-set pillars, change by a single touch the air of these Greek cities and we are at Glastonbury by the tomb of Arthur. The nymph in furred raiment who seduces Hylas is conceived frankly in the spirit of Teutonic romance; her song is of a garden enclosed, such as that with which the old church glass-stainer surrounds the mystic bride of the song of songs. Medea herself has a hundred touches of the medieval sorceress, the sorceress of the Streckelberg or the Blocksberg: her mystic changes are Christabel's. It is precisely this effect, this grace of Hellenism relieved against the sorrow of the Middle Age, which forms the chief motive of *The Earthly Paradise*: with an exquisite dexterity the two threads of sentiment are here interwoven and contrasted. A band of adventurers sets out from Norway, most northerly of northern lands, where the plague is raging—the bell continually ringing as they carry the Sacrament to the sick. Even in Mr Morris's earliest poems snatches of the sweet French tongue had always come with something of Hellenic blitheness and grace. And now it is below the very coast of France, through the fleet of Edward the Third, among the gaily painted medieval sails, that we pass to a reserved fragment of Greece, which by some divine good fortune lingers on in the western sea into the Middle Age. There the stories of *The Earthly Paradise* are told, Greek story and romantic alternating; and for the crew of the *Rose Garland*, coming across the sins of the earlier world with the sign of the cross, and drinking Rhine-wine in Greece, the two worlds of sentiment are confronted.

One characteristic of the pagan spirit the æsthetic poetry has, which is on its surface—the continual suggestion, pensive or passion-ate, of the shortness of life. This is contrasted with the bloom of the world, and gives new seduction to it—the sense of death and the desire of beauty: the desire of beauty quickened by the sense of death.

WORDSWORTH[1]

Some English critics at the beginning of the present century had a great deal to say concerning a distinction, of much importance, as they thought, in the true estimate of poetry, between the *Fancy*, and another more powerful faculty—the *Imagination*. This metaphysical distinction, borrowed originally from the writings of German philosophers, and perhaps not always clearly apprehended by those who talked of it, involved a far deeper and more vital distinction, with which indeed all true criticism more or less directly has to do, the distinction, namely, between higher and lower degrees of intensity in the poet's perception of his subject, and in his concentration of himself upon his work. Of those who dwelt upon the metaphysical distinction between the Fancy and the Imagination, it was Wordsworth who made the most of it, assuming it as the basis for the final classification of his poetical writings; and it is in these writings that the deeper and more vital distinction, which, as I have said, underlies the metaphysical distinction, is most needed, and may best be illustrated.

For nowhere is there so perplexed a mixture as in Wordsworth's own poetry, of work touched with intense and individual power, with work of almost no character at all. He has much conventional sentiment, and some of that insincere poetic diction, against which his most serious critical efforts were directed: the reaction in his political ideas, consequent on the excesses of 1795, makes him, at times, a mere declaimer on moral and social topics; and he seems, sometimes, to force an unwilling pen, and write by rule. By making the most of these blemishes it is possible to obscure the true æsthetic value of his work, just as his life also, a life of much quiet delicacy and independence, might easily be placed in a false focus, and made to appear a somewhat tame theme in illustration of the more obvious parochial virtues. And those who wish to understand his influence, and experience his peculiar savour, must bear with patience the presence of an alien element in Wordsworth's work, which never coalesced with what is really delightful in it, nor underwent his special power. Who that values his writings most has not felt the intrusion there, from time to time, of something tedious and prosaic? Of all poets equally great, he would gain most by a skilfully made anthology. Such a selection would show, in truth, not so much what he was, or to himself or others seemed to be, as what, by the more energetic and fertile quality in his writings, he was ever tending to become. And the mixture in his work, as it actually stands, is so perplexed, that one fears to miss the least promising composition even, lest some precious morsel should be lying hidden within—the few perfect lines, the phrase, the single word perhaps, to which he often works up mechanically through a poem, almost the whole of which may be tame enough. He who thought that in all creative work the larger part was *given* passively, to the recipient mind, who waited so dutifully upon the gift, to whom so large a measure was sometimes given, had his times also of desertion and relapse; and he has permitted the impress of these too to remain in his work. And this duality there—the fitfulness with which the higher qualities manifest themselves in it, gives the effect in his poetry of a power not altogether his own, or under his control, which comes and goes when it will, lifting or lowering a matter, poor in itself; so that that old fancy which made the poet's art an enthusiasm, a form of divine possession, seems almost literally true of him.

This constant suggestion of an absolute duality between higher and lower moods, and the work done in them, stimulating one always to look below the surface, makes the reading of Wordsworth an excellent sort of training towards the things of art and poetry. It begets in those, who, coming across him in youth, can bear him at all, a habit of reading between the lines, a faith in the effect of concentration and collectedness of mind in the right appreciation of poetry, an expectation of things, in this order, coming to one by means of a right discipline of the temper as well as of the intellect. He meets us with the promise that he has much, and something very peculiar, to give us, if we will follow a certain difficult way, and seems to have the secret of a special and privileged state of mind. And those who have undergone his influence, and followed this difficult way, are like people who have passed through some initiation, a *disciplina arcani*, by submitting to which they become able constantly to distinguish in art, speech, feeling, manners, that which is organic, animated, expressive, from that which is only conventional, derivative, inexpressive.

But although the necessity of selecting these precious morsels for oneself is an opportunity for the exercise of Wordsworth's peculiar influence, and induces a kind of just criticism and true estimate of it, yet the purely literary product would have been more excellent, had the writer himself purged away that alien element. How perfect would have been the little treasury, shut between the covers of how thin a book! Let us suppose the desired separation made, the electric thread untwined, the golden pieces, great and small, lying apart together.* What are the peculiarities of this residue? What special sense does Wordsworth exercise, and what instincts does he satisfy? What are the subjects and the motives which in him excite the imaginative faculty? What are the qualities in things and persons which he values, the impression and sense of which he can convey to others, in an extraordinary way?

An intimate consciousness of the expression of natural things, which weighs, listens, penetrates, where the earlier mind passed roughly by, is a large element in the complexion of modern poetry.[3] It has been remarked as a fact in mental history again and again. It reveals itself in many forms; but is strongest and most attractive in what is strongest and most attractive in modern literature. It is exemplified, almost equally, by writers as unlike each other as Senancour and Théophile Gautier: as a singular chapter in the history of the human mind, its growth might be traced from Rousseau to Chateaubriand, from Chateaubriand to Victor Hugo: it has doubtless some latent connexion with those pantheistic theories which locate an intelligent soul in material things, and have largely exercised men's minds in some modern systems of philosophy: it is traceable even in the graver writings of historians: it makes as much difference between ancient and modern landscape art, as there is between the rough masks of an early mosaic and a portrait by Reynolds or Gainsborough. Of this new sense, the writings of Wordsworth are the central and elementary expression: he is more simply and entirely occupied with it than any other poet, though there are fine expressions of precisely the same thing in so different a poet as Shelley. There was in his own character a certain contentment, a sort of inborn religious placidity, seldom found united with a sensibility so mobile as his, which was favourable to the quiet, habitual observation of inanimate, or imperfectly animate, existence. His life of eighty years is divided by no very profoundly felt incidents:[4] its changes are almost wholly inward, and it falls into broad, untroubled, perhaps somewhat monotonous spaces. What it most resembles is the life of one of those early Italian or Flemish painters, who, just because their minds were full of heavenly visions, passed, some of them, the better part of sixty years in quiet, systematic industry. This placid life matured a quite unusual sensibility, really innate in him, to the sights and sounds of the natural world—the flower and its shadow on the stone, the cuckoo and its

* Since this essay was written, such selections have been made, with excellent taste, by Matthew Arnold and Professor Knight.[2]

echo. The poem of *Resolution and Independence* is a storehouse of such records: for its fulness of imagery it may be compared to Keats's *Saint Agnes' Eve*.[5] To read one of his longer pastoral poems for the first time, is like a day spent in a new country: the memory is crowded for a while with its precise and vivid incidents—

> The pliant harebell swinging in the breeze
> On some grey rock;—
>
> The single sheep and the one blasted tree
> And the bleak music from that old stone wall;—
>
> In the meadows and the lower ground
> Was all the sweetness of a common dawn;—
>
> And that green corn all day is rustling in thine ears.

Clear and delicate at once, as he is in the outlining of visible imagery, he is more clear and delicate still, and finely scrupulous, in the noting of sounds; so that he conceives of noble sound as even moulding the human countenance to nobler types, and as something actually 'profaned' by colour, by visible form, or image. He has a power likewise of realising, and conveying to the consciousness of the reader, abstract and elementary impressions—silence, darkness, absolute motionlessness: or, again, the whole complex sentiment of a particular place, the abstract expression of desolation in the long white road, of peacefulness in a particular folding of the hills. In the airy building of the brain, a special day or hour even, comes to have for him a sort of personal identity, a spirit or angel given to it, by which, for its exceptional insight, or the happy light upon it, it has a presence in one's history, and acts there, as a separate power or accomplishment; and he has celebrated in many of his poems the 'efficacious spirit', which, as he says, resides in these 'particular spots' of time.

It is to such a world, and to a world of congruous meditation thereon, that we see him retiring in his but lately published poem of *The Recluse*—taking leave, without much count of costs, of the world of business, of action and ambition, as also of all that for the majority of mankind counts as sensuous enjoyment.*

---

* In Wordsworth's prefatory advertisement to the first edition of *The Prelude*, published in 1850, it is stated that that work was intended to be introductory to *The Recluse*; and that *The Recluse*, if completed, would have consisted of three parts. The second part is 'The Excursion'. The third part was only planned; but the first book of the first part was left in manuscript by Wordsworth—though in manuscript, it is said, in no great condition of forwardness for the printers. This

And so it came about that this sense of a life in natural objects, which in most poetry is but a rhetorical artifice, is with Wordsworth the assertion of what for him is almost literal fact. To him every natural object seemed to possess more or less of a moral or spiritual life, to be capable of a companionship with man, full of expression, of inexplicable affinities and delicacies of intercourse. An emanation, a particular spirit, belonged, not to the moving leaves or water only, but to the distant peak of the hills arising suddenly, by some change of perspective, above the nearer horizon, to the passing space of light across the plain, to the lichened Druidic stone even, for a certain weird fellowship in it with the moods of men. It was like a 'survival', in the peculiar intellectual temperament of a man of letters at the end of the eighteenth century, of that primitive condition, which some philosophers have traced in the general history of human culture, wherein all outward objects alike, including even the works of men's hands, were believed to be endowed with animation, and the world

---

book, now for the first time printed *in extenso* (a very noble passage from it found place in that prose advertisement to *The Excursion*), is included in the latest edition of Wordsworth by Mr John Morley. It was well worth adding to the poet's great bequest to English literature. A true student of his work, who has formulated for himself what he supposes to be the leading characteristics of Wordsworth's genius, will feel, we think, lively interest in testing them by the various fine passages in what is here presented for the first time. Let the following serve for a sample:—

> Thickets full of songsters, and the voice
> Of lordly birds, an unexpected sound
> Heard now and then from morn to latest eve,
> Admonishing the man who walks below
> Of solitude and silence in the sky:—
> These have we, and a thousand nooks of earth
> Have also these, but nowhere else is found,
> Nowhere (or is it fancy?) can be found
> The one sensation that is here; 'tis here,
> Here as it found its way into my heart
> In childhood, here as it abides by day,
> By night, here only; or in chosen minds
> That take it with them hence, where'er they go.
> —'Tis, but I cannot name it, 'tis the sense
> Of majesty, and beauty, and repose,
> A blended holiness of earth and sky,
> Something that makes this individual spot,
> This small abiding-place of many men,
> A termination, and a last retreat,
> A centre, come from wheresoe'er you will,
> A whole without dependence or defect,
> Made for itself, and happy in itself,
> Perfect contentment, Unity entire.

was 'full of souls'—that mood in which the old Greek gods were first begotten, and which had many strange aftergrowths.[6]

In the early ages, this belief, delightful as its effects on poetry often are, was but the result of a crude intelligence. But, in Wordsworth, such power of seeing life, such perception of a soul, in inanimate things, came of an exceptional susceptibility to the impressions of eye and ear, and was, in its essence, a kind of sensuousness. At least, it is only in a temperament exceptionally susceptible on the sensuous side, that this sense of the expressiveness of outward things comes to be so large a part of life. That he awakened 'a sort of thought in sense', is Shelley's just estimate of this element in Wordsworth's poetry.

And it was through nature, thus ennobled by a semblance of passion and thought, that he approached the spectacle of human life. Human life, indeed, is for him, at first, only an additional, accidental grace on an expressive landscape. When he thought of man, it was of man as in the presence and under the influence of these effective natural objects, and linked to them by many associations. The close connexion of man with natural objects, the habitual association of his thoughts and feelings with a particular spot of earth, has sometimes seemed to degrade those who are subject to its influence, as if it did but reinforce that physical connexion of our nature with the actual lime and clay of the soil, which is always drawing us nearer to our end. But for Wordsworth, these influences tended to the dignity of human nature, because they tended to tranquillise it. By raising nature to the level of human thought he gives it power and expression: he subdues man to the level of nature, and gives him thereby a certain breadth and coolness and solemnity. The leech-gatherer on the moor, the woman 'stepping westward', are for him natural objects, almost in the same sense as the aged thorn, or the lichened rock on the heath. In this sense the leader of the 'Lake School', in spite of an earnest pre-occupation with man, his thoughts, his destiny, is the poet of nature. And of nature, after all, in its modesty. The English lake country has, of course, its grandeurs. But the peculiar function of Wordsworth's genius, as carrying in it a power to open out the soul of apparently little or familiar things, would have found its true test had he become the poet of Surrey, say! and the prophet of its life. The glories of Italy and Switzerland, though he did write a little about them, had too potent a material life of their own to serve greatly his poetic purpose.

Religious sentiment, consecrating the affections and natural regrets of the human heart, above all, that pitiful awe and care for the perishing human clay, of which relic-worship is but the corruption, has always had much to do with localities, with the thoughts which attach themselves to actual scenes and places. Now what is true of it everywhere, is truest of it in those secluded valleys where one generation after another maintains the same abiding-place; and it was on this side, that Wordsworth apprehended religion most strongly. Consisting, as it did so much, in the recognition of local sanctities, in the habit of connecting the stones and trees of a particular spot of earth with the great events of life, till the low walls, the green mounds, the half-obliterated epitaphs seemed full of voices, and a sort of natural oracles, the very religion of these people of the dales appeared but as another link between them and the earth, and was literally a religion of nature. It tranquillised them by bringing them under the placid rule of traditional and narrowly localised observances. 'Grave livers', they seemed to him, under this aspect, with stately speech, and something of that natural dignity of manners, which underlies the highest courtesy.

And, seeing man thus as a part of nature, elevated and solemnised in proportion as his daily life and occupations brought him into companionship with permanent natural objects, his very religion forming new links for him with the narrow limits of the valley, the low vaults of his church, the rough stones of his home, made intense for him now with profound sentiment, Wordsworth was able to appreciate passion in the lowly. He chooses to depict people from humble life, because, being nearer to nature than others, they are on the whole more impassioned, certainly more direct in their expression of passion, than other men: it is for this direct expression of passion, that he values their humble words. In much that he said in exaltation of rural life, he was but pleading indirectly for that sincerity, that perfect fidelity to one's own inward presentations, to the precise features of the picture within, without which any profound poetry is impossible. It was not for their tameness, but for this passionate sincerity, that he chose incidents and situations from common life, 'related in a selection of language really used by men'. He constantly endeavours to bring his language near to the real language of men: to the real language of men, however, not on the dead level of their ordinary intercourse, but in select moments of vivid sensation, when this language is winnowed and ennobled by excitement. There are poets who have chosen rural life as their subject, for the sake of its passionless repose, and times when Wordsworth himself extols the mere calm and dispassionate survey of things as the highest aim of poetical culture. But it was not for such passionless calm that he preferred the scenes of pastoral life; and the meditative poet, sheltering himself, as it might seem, from the agitations of the outward world, is in reality only clearing the scene for the great exhibitions of emotion, and what he values most is the almost elementary expression of elementary feelings.

And so he has much for those who value highly the concentrated presentment of passion, who appraise men and women by their susceptibility to it, and art and poetry as they afford the spectacle of it. Breaking from time to time into the pensive spectacle of their daily toil, their occupations near to nature, come those great elementary feelings, lifting and solemnising their language and giving it a natural music. The great, distinguishing passion came to Michael by the sheepfold, to Ruth by the wayside, adding these humble children of the furrow to the true aristocracy of passionate souls. In this respect, Wordsworth's work resembles most that of George Sand, in those of her novels which depict country life. With a penetrative pathos, which puts him in the same rank with the masters of the sentiment of pity in literature, with Meinhold and Victor Hugo, he collects all the traces of vivid excitement which were to be found in that pastoral world— the girl who rung her father's knell; the unborn infant feeling about its mother's heart; the instinctive touches of children; the sorrows of the wild creatures, even—their home-sickness, their strange yearnings; the tales of passionate regret that hang by a ruined farm-building, a heap of stones, a deserted sheepfold; that gay, false, adventurous, outer world, which breaks in from time to time to bewilder and deflower these quiet homes; not 'passionate sorrow' only, for the overthrow of the soul's beauty, but the loss of, or carelessness for personal beauty even, in those whom men have wronged— their pathetic wanness; the sailor 'who, in his heart, was half a shepherd on the stormy seas'; the wild woman teaching her child to pray for her betrayer; incidents like the making of the shepherd's staff, or that of the young boy laying the first stone of the sheepfold; —all the pathetic episodes of their humble existence, their longing, their wonder at fortune, their poor pathetic pleasures, like the pleasures of children, won so hardly in the struggle for bare existence; their yearning towards each other, in their darkened houses, or at their early toil. A sort of biblical depth and solemnity hangs over this strange, new, passionate, pastoral world, of which he first raised the image, and the reflection of which some of our best modern fiction has caught from him.

He pondered much over the philosophy of his poetry, and reading deeply in the history of his own mind, seems at times to have passed the borders of a world of strange speculations, inconsistent enough, had he cared to note such inconsistencies, with those traditional beliefs, which were otherwise the object of his devout acceptance.

Thinking of the high value he set upon customariness, upon all that is habitual, local, rooted in the ground, in matters of religious senti-ment, you might sometimes regard him as one tethered down to a world, refined and peaceful indeed, but with no broad outlook, a world protected, but somewhat narrowed, by the influence of received ideas. But he is at times also something very different from this, and something much bolder. A chance expression is overheard and placed in a new connexion, the sudden memory of a thing long past occurs to him, a distant object is relieved for a while by a random gleam of light—accidents turning up for a moment what lies below the sur-face of our immediate experience—and he passes from the humble graves and lowly arches of 'the little rock-like pile' of a West-moreland church, on bold trains of speculative thought, and comes, from point to point, into strange contact with thoughts which have visited, from time to time, far more venturesome, perhaps errant, spirits.

He had pondered deeply, for instance, on those strange reminis-cences and forebodings, which seem to make our lives stretch before and behind us, beyond where we can see or touch anything, or trace the lines of connexion. Following the soul, backwards and forwards, on these endless ways, his sense of man's dim, potential powers became a pledge to him, indeed, of a future life, but carried him back also to that mysterious notion of an earlier state of existence—the fancy of the Platonists—the old heresy of Origen. It was in this mood that he conceived those oft-reiterated regrets for a half-ideal childhood, when the relics of Paradise still clung about the soul—a childhood, as it seemed, full of the fruits of old age, lost for all, in a degree, in the passing away of the youth of the world, lost for each one, over again, in the passing away of actual youth. It is this ideal childhood which he celebrates in his famous *Ode on the Recollections of Childhood*, and some other poems which may be grouped around it, such as the lines on *Tintern Abbey*, and something like what he describes was actually truer of himself than he seems to have understood; for his own most delightful poems were really the instinctive productions of earlier life, and most surely for him, 'the first diviner influence of this world' passed away, more and more completely, in his contact with experience.

Sometimes as he dwelt upon those moments of profound, imaginative power, in which the outward object appears to take colour and expression, a new nature almost, from the prompting of the observant mind, the actual world would, as it were, dissolve and detach itself, flake by flake, and he himself seemed to be the creator, and when he would the destroyer, of the world in which he lived—

that old isolating thought of many a brain-sick mystic of ancient and modern times.

At other times, again, in those periods of intense susceptibility, in which he appeared to himself as but the passive recipient of external influences, he was attracted by the thought of a spirit of life in outward things, a single, all-pervading mind in them, of which man, and even the poet's imaginative energy, are but moments—that old dream of the *anima mundi*, the mother of all things and their grave, in which some had desired to lose themselves, and others had become indifferent to the distinctions of good and evil. It would come, sometimes, like the sign of the *macrocosm* to Faust in his cell: the network of man and nature was seen to be pervaded by a common, universal life: a new, bold thought lifted him above the furrow, above the green turf of the Westmoreland churchyard, to a world altogether different in its vagueness and vastness, and the narrow glen was full of the brooding power of one universal spirit.

And so he has something, also, for those who feel the fascination of bold speculative ideas, who are really capable of rising upon them to conditions of poetical thought. He uses them, indeed, always with a very fine apprehension of the limits within which alone philosophical imaginings have any place in true poetry; and using them only for poetical purposes, is not too careful even to make them consistent with each other. To him, theories which for other men bring a world of technical diction, brought perfect form and expression, as in those two lofty books of *The Prelude*, which describe the decay and the restoration of Imagination and Taste. Skirting the borders of this world of bewildering heights and depths, he got but the first exciting influence of it, that joyful enthusiasm which great imaginative theories prompt, when the mind first comes to have an understanding of them; and it is not under the influence of these thoughts that his poetry becomes tedious or loses its blitheness. He keeps them, too, always within certain ethical bounds, so that no word of his could offend the simplest of those simple souls which are always the largest portion of mankind. But it is, nevertheless, the contact of these thoughts, the speculative boldness in them, which constitutes, at least for some minds, the secret attraction of much of his best poetry—the sudden passage from lowly thoughts and places to the majestic forms of philosophical imagination, the play of these forms over a world so different, enlarging so strangely the bounds of its humble churchyards, and breaking such a wild light on the graves of christened children.

And these moods always brought with them faultless expression.

In regard to expression, as with feeling and thought, the duality of the higher and lower moods was absolute. It belonged to the higher, the imaginative mood, and was the pledge of its reality, to bring the appropriate language with it. In him, when the really poetical motive worked at all, it united, with absolute justice, the word and the idea; each, in the imaginative flame, becoming inseparably one with the other, by that fusion of matter and form, which is the characteristic of the highest poetical expression. His words are themselves thought and feeling; not eloquent, or musical words merely, but that sort of creative language which carries the reality of what it depicts, directly, to the consciousness.

The music of mere metre performs but a limited, yet a very peculiar and subtly ascertained function, in Wordsworth's poetry. With him, metre is but an additional grace, accessory to that deeper music of words and sounds, that moving power, which they exercise in the nobler prose no less than in formal poetry. It is a sedative to that excitement, an excitement sometimes almost painful, under which the language, alike of poetry and prose, attains a rhythmical power, independent of metrical combination, and dependent rather on some subtle adjustment of the elementary sounds of words themselves to the image or feeling they convey. Yet some of his pieces, pieces prompted by a sort of half-playful mysticism, like the *Daffodils* and *The Two April Mornings*, are distinguished by a certain quaint gaiety of metre, and rival by their perfect execution, in this respect, similar pieces among our own Elizabethan, or contemporary French poetry. And those who take up these poems after an interval of months, or years perhaps, may be surprised at finding how well old favourites wear, how their strange, inventive turns of diction or thought still send through them the old feeling of surprise. Those who lived about Wordsworth were all great lovers of the older English literature, and oftentimes there came out in him a noticeable likeness to our earlier poets. He quotes unconsciously, but with new power of meaning, a clause from one of Shakespeare's sonnets; and, as with some other men's most famous work, the *Ode on the Recollections of Childhood* had its anticipator.* He drew something too from the unconscious mysticism of the old English language itself, drawing out the inward significance of its racy idiom, and the not wholly unconscious poetry of the language used by the simplest people under strong excitement— language, therefore, at its origin.

The office of the poet is not that of the moralist, and the first aim

* Henry Vaughan, in *The Retreat.*

of Wordsworth's poetry is to give the reader a peculiar kind of pleasure. But through his poetry, and through this pleasure in it, he does actually convey to the reader an extraordinary wisdom in the things of practice. One lesson, if men must have lessons, he conveys more clearly than all, the supreme importance of contemplation in the conduct of life.

Contemplation—impassioned contemplation—that, is with Wordsworth the end-in-itself, the perfect end. We see the majority of mankind going most often to definite ends, lower or higher ends, as their own insticts may determine; but the end may never be attained, and the means not be quite the right means, great ends and little ones alike being, for the most part, distant, and the ways to them, in this dim world, somewhat vague. Meantime, to higher or lower ends, they move too often with something of a sad countenance, with hurried and ignoble gait, becoming, unconsciously, something like thorns, in their anxiety to bear grapes; it being possible for people, in the pursuit of even great ends, to become themselves thin and impoverished in spirit and temper, thus diminishing the sum of perfection in the world, at its very sources. We understand this when it is a question of mean, or of intensely selfish ends—of Grandet, or Javert. We think it bad morality to say that the end justifies the means, and we know how false to all higher conceptions of the religious life is the type of one who is ready to do evil that good may come. We contrast with such dark, mistaken eagerness, a type like that of Saint Catherine of Siena, who made the means to her ends so attractive, that she has won for herself an undying place in the *House Beautiful*, not by her rectitude of soul only, but by its 'fairness'—by those quite different qualities which commend themselves to the poet and the artist.

Yet, for most of us, the conception of means and ends covers the whole of life, and is the exclusive type or figure under which we represent our lives to ourselves. Such a figure, reducing all things to machinery, though it has on its side the authority of that old Greek moralist who has fixed for succeeding generations the outline of the theory of right living, is too like a mere picture or description of men's lives as we actually find them, to be the basis of the higher ethics. It covers the meanness of men's daily lives, and much of the dexterity and the vigour with which they pursue what may seem to them the good of themselves or of others; but not the intangible perfection of those whose ideal is rather in *being* than in *doing*—not those *manners* which are, in the deepest as in the simplest sense, *morals*, and without which one cannot so much as offer a cup of water to a poor man without offence—not the part of 'antique Rachel', sitting in the company of Beatrice; and even the moralist might well endeavour rather to withdraw men from the too exclusive consideration of means and ends, in life.

Against this predominance of machinery in our existence, Wordsworth's poetry, like all great art and poetry, is a continual protest. Justify rather the end by the means, it seems to say: whatever may become of the fruit, make sure of the flowers and the leaves. It was justly said, therefore, by one who had meditated very profoundly on the true relation of means to ends in life, and on the distinction between what is desirable in itself and what is desirable only as machinery, that when the battle which he and his friends were waging had been won, the world would need more than ever those qualities which Wordsworth was keeping alive and nourishing.*

That the end of life is not action but contemplation—*being* as distinct from *doing*—a certain disposition of the mind: is, in some shape or other, the principle of all the higher morality. In poetry, in art, if you enter into their true spirit at all, you touch this principle, in a measure: these, by their very sterility, are a type of beholding for the mere joy of beholding. To treat life in the spirit of art, is to make life a thing in which means and ends are identified: to encourage such treatment, the true moral significance of art and poetry. Wordsworth, and other poets who have been like him in ancient or more recent times, are the masters, the experts, in this art of impassioned contemplation. Their work is, not to teach lessons, or enforce rules, or even to stimulate us to noble ends; but to withdraw the thoughts for a little while from the mere machinery of life, to fix them, with appropriate emotions, on the spectacle of those great facts in man's existence which no machinery affects, 'on the great and universal passions of men, the most general and interesting of their occupations, and the entire world of nature',—on 'the operations of the elements and the appearances of the visible universe, on storm and sunshine, on the revolutions of the seasons, on cold and heat, on loss of friends and kindred, on injuries and resentments, on gratitude and hope, on fear and sorrow'. To witness this spectacle with appropriate emotions is the aim of all culture; and of these emotions poetry like Wordsworth's is a great nourisher and stimulant. He seees nature full of sentiment and excitement; he sees men and women as parts of nature, passionate, excited, in strange grouping and connexion with the grandeur and beauty of the natural world:—images, in his own words, 'of man suffering, amid awful forms and powers'.

* See an interesting paper, by Mr John Morley, on 'The Death of Mr Mill', *Fortnightly Review,* June 1873.

Such is the figure of the more powerful and original poet, hidden away, in part, under those weaker elements in Wordsworth's poetry, which for some minds determine their entire character; a poet somewhat bolder and more passionate than might at first sight be supposed, but not too bold for true poetical taste; an unimpassioned writer, you might sometimes fancy, yet thinking the chief aim, in life and art alike, to be a certain deep emotion; seeking most often the great elementary passions in lowly places; having at least this condition of all impassioned work, that he aims always at an absolute sincerity of feeling and diction, so that he is the true forerunner of the deepest and most passionate poetry of our own day; yet going back also, with something of a protest against the conventional fervour of much of the poetry popular in his own time, to those older English poets, whose unconscious likeness often comes out in him.

MEASURE FOR MEASURE[1]

In *Measure for Measure*, as in some other of his plays, Shakespeare has remodelled an earlier and somewhat rough composition to 'finer issues', suffering much to remain as it had come from the less skilful hand, and not raising the whole of his work to an equal degree of intensity. Hence perhaps some of that depth and weightiness which make this play so impressive, as with the true seal of experience, like a fragment of life itself, rough and disjointed indeed, but forced to yield in places its profounder meaning. In *Measure for Measure*, in contrast with the flawless execution of *Romeo and Juliet*, Shakespeare has spent his art in just enough modification of the scheme of the older play to make it exponent of this purpose, adapting its terrible essential incidents, so that Coleridge found it the only painful work among Shakespeare's dramas,[2] and leaving for the reader of to-day more than the usual number of difficult expressions; but infusing a lavish colour and a profound significance into it, so that under his touch certain select portions of it rise far above the level of all but his own best poetry, and working out of it a morality so characteristic that the play might well pass for the central expression of his moral judgments. It remains a comedy, as indeed is congruous with the bland, half-humorous equity which informs the whole composition, sinking from the heights of sorrow and terror into the rough scheme of the earlier piece; yet it is hardly less full of what is really tragic in man's existence than if Claudio had indeed 'stooped to death'. Even the humorous concluding scenes have traits of special grace, retaining in less emphatic passages a stray line or word of power, as it seems, so that we watch to the end for the traces where the nobler hand has glanced along, leaving its vestiges, as if accidentally or wastefully, in the rising of the style.

The interest of *Measure for Measure*, therefore, is partly that of an old story told over again. We measure with curiosity that variety of resources which has enabled Shakespeare to refashion the original material with a higher motive; adding to the intricacy of the piece, yet so modifying its structure as to give the whole almost the unity of a single scene; lending, by the light of a philosophy which dwells much on what is complex and subtle in our nature, a true human propriety to its strange and unexpected turns of feeling and character, to incidents so difficult as the fall of Angelo, and the subsequent reconciliation of Isabella, so that she pleads successfully for his life. It was from Whetstone, a contemporary English writer, that Shakespeare derived the outline of Cinthio's 'rare history' of *Promos and Cassandra*, one of that numerous class of Italian stories, like Boccaccio's *Tancred of Salerno*, in which the mere energy of southern passion has everything its own way, and which, though they may repel many a northern reader by a certain crudity in their colouring, seem to have been full of fascination for the Elizabethan age. This story, as it appears in Whetstone's endless comedy, is almost as rough as the roughest episode of actual criminal life. But the play seems never to have been acted, and some time after its publication Whetstone himself turned the thing into a tale, included in his *Heptameron of Civil Discourses*, where it still figures as a genuine piece, with touches of undesigned poetry, a quaint field-flower here and there of diction or sentiment, the whole strung up to an effective brevity, and with the fragrance of that admirable age of literature all about it. Here, then, there is something of the original Italian colour: in this narrative Shakespeare may well have caught the first glimpse of a composition with nobler proportions; and some artless sketch from his own hand, perhaps, putting together his first impressions, insinuated itself between Whetstone's work and the play as we actually read it. Out of these insignificant sources Shakespeare's play rises, full of solemn expression, and with a profoundly designed beauty, the new body of a higher, though sometimes remote and difficult poetry, escaping from the imperfect relics of the old story, yet not wholly transformed, and even as it stands but the preparation only, we might think, of a still more imposing design. For once we have in it a real example of that sort of writing which is sometimes described as *suggestive*, and which by the help of certain subtly calculated hints only, brings into distinct shape the reader's own half-developed imaginings. Often the quality is attributed to writing merely vague and unrealised, but in *Measure for Measure*, quite certainly, Shakespeare has directed the attention of sympathetic readers along certain channels of meditation beyond the immediate scope of his work.

Measure for Measure, therefore, by the quality of these higher designs, woven by his strange magic on a texture of poorer quality, is hardly less indicative than *Hamlet* even, of Shakespeare's reason, of his power of mortal interpretation. It deals, not like *Hamlet* with the problems which beset one of exceptional temperament, but with mere human nature. It brings before us a group of persons, attractive, full of desire, vessels of the genial, seed-bearing powers of nature, a gaudy existence flowering out over the old court and city of Vienna, a spectacle of the fulness and pride of life which to some may seem to touch the verge of wantonness. Behind this group of people, behind their various action, Shakespeare inspires in us the sense of a strong tyranny of nature and circumstance. Then what shall there be on this side of it—on our side, the spectators' side, of this painted screen, with its puppets who are really glad or sorry all the time? what philosophy of life, what sort of equity?

Stimulated to read more carefully by Shakespeare's own profounder touches, the reader will note the vivid reality, the subtle interchange of light and shade, the strongly contrasted characters of this group of persons, passing across the stage so quickly. The slightest of them is at least not ill-natured: the meanest of them can put forth a plea for existence—*Truly, sir, I am a poor fellow that would live!*—they are never sure of themselves, even in the strong tower of a cold unimpressible nature: they are capable of many friendships and of a true dignity in danger, giving each other a sympathetic, if transitory, regret—one sorry that another 'should be foolishly lost at a game of tick-tack'. Words which seem to exhaust man's deepest sentiment concerning death and life are put on the lips of a gilded, witless youth; and the saintly Isabella feels fire creep along her, kindling her tongue to eloquence at the suggestion of shame. In places the shadow deepens: death intrudes itself on the scene, as among other things 'a greater disguiser', blanching the features of youth and spoiling its goodly hair, touching the fine Claudio even with its disgraceful associations. As in Orcagna's fresco at Pisa, it comes capriciously, giving many and long reprieves to Barnardine, who has been waiting for it nine years in prison, taking another thence by fever, another by mistake of judgment, embracing others in the midst of their music and song. The little mirror of existence, which reflects to each for a moment the stage on which he plays, is broken at last by a capricious accident; while all alike, in their yearning for untasted enjoyment, are really discounting their days, grasping so hastily and accepting so inexactly the precious pieces. The Duke's quaint but excellent moralising at the beginning of the third act does but express, like the chorus of a Greek play, the spirit of the passing incidents. To him in Shakespeare's play, to a few here and there in the actual world, this strange practical paradox of our life, so unwise in its eager haste, reveals itself in all its clearness.

The Duke disguised as a friar, with his curious moralising on life and death, and Isabella in her first mood of renunciation, a thing

'ensky'd and sainted', come with the quiet of the cloister as a relief to
this lust and pride of life: like some grey monastic picture hung on
the wall of a gaudy room, their presence cools the heated air of the
piece. For a moment we are within the placid conventual walls,
whither they fancy at first that the Duke has come as a man crossed
in love, with Friar Thomas and Friar Peter, calling each other by
their homely, English names, or at the nunnery among the novices,
with their little limited privileges, where

> If you speak you must not show your face,
> Or if you show your face you must not speak.

Not less precious for this relief in the general structure of the piece,
than for its own peculiar graces is the episode of Mariana, a creature
wholly of Shakespeare's invention, told, by way of interlude, in subdued prose. The moated grange, with its dejected mistress, its long,
listless, discontented days, where we hear only the voice of a boy
broken off suddenly in the midst of one of the loveliest songs of
Shakespeare, or of Shakespeare's school,* is the pleasantest of many
glimpses we get here of pleasant places—the field without the town,
Angelo's garden-house, the consecrated fountain. Indirectly it has
suggested two of the most perfect compositions among the poetry of
our own generation.[3] Again it is a picture within a picture, but with
fainter lines and a greyer atmosphere: we have here the same passions,
the same wrongs, the same continuance of affection, the same crying
out upon death, as in the nearer and larger piece, though softened,
and reduced to the mood of a more dreamy scene.

Of Angelo we may feel at first sight inclined to say only *guarda e
passa!* or to ask whether he is indeed psychologically possible. In the
old story, he figures as an embodiment of pure and unmodified evil,
like 'Hyliogabalus of Rome or Denis of Sicyll'. But the embodiment
of pure evil is no proper subject of art, and Shakespeare, in the spirit
of a philosophy which dwells much on the complications of outward
circumstance with men's inclinations, turns into a subtle study in
casuistry this incident of the austere judge fallen suddenly into utmost
corruption by a momentary contact with supreme purity. But the
main interest in *Measure for Measure* is not, as in *Promos and Cassandra*,
in the relation of Isabella and Angelo, but rather in the relation of
Claudio and Isabella.

Greek tragedy in some of its noblest products has taken for its
theme the love of a sister, a sentiment unimpassioned indeed, purify-
ing by the very spectacle of its passionlessness, but capable of a fierce

* Fletcher, in the *Bloody Brother*, gives the rest of it.

and almost animal strength if informed for a moment by pity and regret. At first Isabella comes upon the scene as a tranquillising influence in it. But Shakespeare, in the development of the action, brings quite different and unexpected qualities out of her. It is his characteristic poetry to expose this cold, chastened personality, respected even by the worldly Lucio as 'something ensky'd and sainted, and almost an immortal spirit', to two sharp, shameful trials, and wring out of her a fiery, revealing eloquence. Thrown into the terrible dilemma of the piece, called upon to sacrifice that cloistral whiteness to sisterly affection, become in a moment the ground of strong, contending passions, she develops a new character and shows herself suddenly of kindred with those strangely conceived women, like Webster's Vittoria, who unite to a seductive sweetness something of a dangerous and tigerlike changefulness of feeling. The swift, vindictive anger leaps, like a white flame, into this white spirit, and, stripped in a moment of all convention, she stands before us clear, detached, columnar, among the tender frailties of the piece. Cassandra, the original of Isabella in Whetstone's tale, with the purpose of the Roman Lucretia in her mind, yields gracefully enough to the conditions of her brother's safety; and to the lighter reader of Shakespeare there may seem something harshly conceived, or psychologically impossible even, in the suddenness of the change wrought in her, as Claudio welcomes for a moment the chance of life through her compliance with Angelo's will, and he may have a sense here of flagging skill, as in words less finely handled than in the preceding scene. The play, though still not without traces of nobler handiwork, sinks down, as we know, at last into almost homely comedy, and it might be supposed that just here the grander manner deserted it. But the skill with which Isabella plays upon Claudio's well-recognised sense of honour, and endeavours by means of that to insure him beforehand from the acceptance of life on baser terms, indicates no coming laxity of hand just in this place. It was rather that there rose in Shakespeare's conception, as there may for the reader, as there certainly would in any good acting of the part, something of that terror, the seeking for which is one of the notes of romanticism in Shakespeare and his circle. The stream of ardent natural affection, poured as sudden hatred upon the youth condemned to die, adds an additional note of expression to the horror of the prison where so much of the scene takes place. It is not here only that Shakespeare has conceived of such extreme anger and pity as putting a sort of genius into simple women, so that their 'lips drop eloquence', and their intuitions interpret that which is often too hard or fine for manlier reason; and it is Isabella with her grand imaginative diction, and that poetry laid upon the 'prone and speechless dialect' there is in mere youth itself, who gives utterance to the equity, the finer judgments of the piece on men and things.

From behind this group with its subtle lights and shades, its poetry, its impressive contrasts, Shakespeare, as I said, conveys to us a strong sense of the tyranny of nature and circumstance over human action.[4] The most powerful expressions of this side of experience might be found here. The bloodless, impassible temperament does but wait for its opportunity, for the almost accidental coherence of time with place, and place with wishing, to annul its long and patient discipline, and become in a moment the very opposite of that which under ordinary conditions it seemed to be, even to itself. The mere resolute self-assertion of the blood brings to others special temptations, temptations which, as defects or over-growths, lie in the very qualities which make them otherwise imposing or attractive; the very advantage of men's gifts of intellect or sentiment being dependent on a balance in their use so delicate that men hardly maintain it always. Something also must be conceded to influences merely physical, to the complexion of the heavens, the skyey influences, shifting as the stars shift; as something also to the mere caprice of men exercised over each other in the dispensations of social or political order, to the chance which makes the life or death of Claudio dependent on Angelo's will.

The many veins of thought which render the poetry of this play so weighty and impressive unite in the image of Claudio, a flowerlike young man, whom, prompted by a few hints from Shakespeare, the imagination easily clothes with all the bravery of youth, as he crosses the stage before us on his way to death, coming so hastily to the end of his pilgrimage. Set in the horrible blackness of the prison, with its various forms of unsightly death, this flower seems the braver. Fallen by 'prompture of the blood', the victim of a suddenly revived law against the common fault of youth like his, he finds his life forfeited as if by the chance of a lottery. With that instinctive clinging to life, which breaks through the subtlest casuistries of monk or sage apologising for an early death, he welcomes for a moment the chance of life through his sister's shame, though he revolts hardly less from the notion of perpetual imprisonment so repulsive to the buoyant energy of youth. Familiarised, by the words alike of friends and the indifferent, to the thought of death, he becomes gentle and subdued indeed, yet more perhaps through pride than real resignation, and would go down to darkness at last hard and unblinded. Called upon suddenly to encounter his fate, looking with keen and resolute profile straight before him, he gives utterance to some of the central truths of human feeling, the sincere, concentrated expression of the recoiling flesh.

Thoughts as profound and poetical as Hamlet's arise in him; and but
for the accidental arrest of sentence he would descend into the dust, a
mere gilded, idle flower of youth indeed, but with what are perhaps
the most eloquent of all Shakespeare's words upon his lips.

As Shakespeare in *Measure for Measure* has refashioned, after a nobler
pattern, materials already at hand, so that the relics of other men's
poetry are incorporated into his perfect work, so traces of the old
'morality', that early form of dramatic composition which had for its
function the inculcating of some moral theme, survive in it also, and
give it a peculiar ethical interest. This ethical interest, though it can
escape no attentive reader, yet, in accordance with that artistic law
which demands the predominance of form everywhere over the mere
matter or subject handled, is not to be wholly separated from the
special circumstances, necessities, embarrassments, of these particular
dramatic persons. The old 'moralities' exemplified most often some
rough-and-ready lesson. Here the very intricacy and subtlety of the
moral world itself, the difficulty of seizing the true relations of so
complex a material, the difficulty of just judgment, of judgment that
shall not be unjust, are the lessons conveyed. Even in Whetstone's old
story this peculiar vein of moralising comes to the surface: even there,
we notice the tendency to dwell on mixed motives, the contending
issues of action, the presence of virtues and vices alike in unexpected
places, on 'the hard choice of two evils', on the 'imprisoning' of men's
'real intents'. *Measure for Measure* is full of expressions drawn from a
profound experience of these casuistries, and that ethical interest
becomes predominant in it: it is no longer *Promos and Cassandra*, but
Measure for Measure, its new name expressly suggesting the subject of
poetical justice. The action of the play, like the action of life itself for the
keener observer, develops in us the conception of this poetical justice,
and the yearning to realise it, the true justice of which Angelo knows
nothing, because it lies for the most part beyond the limits of any
acknowledged law. The idea of justice involves the idea of rights.
But at bottom rights are equivalent to that which really is, to facts;
and the recognition of his rights therefore, the justice he requires of
our hands, or our thoughts, is the recognition of that which the person,
in his inmost nature, really is; and as sympathy alone can discover
that which really is in matters of feeling and thought, true justice is in
its essence a finer knowledge through love.

> 'Tis very pregnant:
> The jewel that we find we stoop and take it,
> Because we see it; but what we do not see
> We tread upon, and never think of it.

It is for this finer justice, a justice based on a more delicate appreciation of the true conditions of men and things, a true respect of persons in our estimate of actions, that the people in *Measure for Measure* cry out as they pass before us; and as the poetry of this play is full of the peculiarities of Shakespeare's poetry, so in its ethics it is an epitome of Shakespeare's moral judgments. They are the moral judgments of an observer, of one who sits as a spectator, and knows how the threads in the design before him hold together under the surface: they are the judgments of the humourist also, who follows with a half-amused but always pitiful sympathy, the various ways of human disposition, and sees less distance than ordinary men between what are called respectively great and little things. It is not always that poetry can be the exponent of morality; but it is this aspect of morals which it represents most naturally, for this true justice is dependent on just those finer appreciations which poetry cultivates in us the power of making, those peculiar valuations of action and its effect which poetry actually requires.

CHARLES LAMB[1]

Those English critics who at the beginning of the present century introduced from Germany, together with some other subtleties of thought transplanted hither not without advantage, the distinction between the *Fancy* and the *Imagination*, made much also of the cognate distinction between *Wit* and *Humour*, between that unreal and transitory mirth, which is as the crackling of thorns under the pot, and the laughter which blends with tears and even with the sublimities of the imagination, and which, in its most exquisite motives, is one with pity—the laughter of the comedies of Shakespeare, hardly less expressive than his moods of seriousness or solemnity, of that deeply stirred soul of sympathy in him, as flowing from which both tears and laughter are alike genuine and contagious.

This distinction between wit and humour, Coleridge and other kindred critics applied, with much effect, in their studies of some of our older English writers. And as the distinction between imagination and fancy, made popular by Wordsworth, found its best justification in certain essential differences of stuff in Wordsworth's own writings, so this other critical distinction, between wit and humour, finds a sort of visible interpretation and instance in the character and writings of Charles Lamb;—one who lived more consistently than most writers among subtle literary theories, and whose remains are still full of curious interest for the student of literature as a fine art.

The author of the *English Humourists of the Eighteenth Century*, coming to the humourists of the nineteenth, would have found, as is true pre-eminently of Thackeray himself, the springs of pity in them deepened by the deeper subjectivity, the intenser and closer living with itself, which is characteristic of the temper of the later generation; and therewith, the mirth also, from the amalgam of which with pity humour proceeds, has become, in Charles Dickens, for example, freer and more boisterous.

To this more high-pitched feeling, since predominant in our literature, the writings of Charles Lamb, whose life occupies the last quarter of the eighteenth century and the first quarter of the nineteenth, are a transition; and such union of grave, of terrible even, with gay, we may note in the circumstances of his life, as reflected thence into his work. We catch the aroma of a singular, homely sweetness about his first years, spent on Thames' side, amid the red bricks and terrraced gardens, with their rich historical memories of old-fashioned legal London. Just above the poorer class, deprived, as he says, of the 'sweet food of academic institution', he is fortunate enough to be reared in the classical languages at an ancient school, where he becomes the companion of Coleridge, as at a later period he was his enthusiastic disciple. So far, the years go by with less than the usual share of boyish difficulties; protected, one fancies, seeing what he was afterwards, by some attraction of temper in the quaint child, small and delicate, with a certain Jewish expression in his clear, brown complexion, eyes not precisely of the same colour, and a slow walk adding to the staidness of his figure; and whose infirmity of speech, increased by agitation, is partly engaging.

And the cheerfulness of all this, of the mere aspect of Lamb's quiet subsequent life also, might make the more superficial reader think of him as in himself something slight, and of his mirth as cheaply bought. Yet we know that beneath this blithe surface there was something of the fateful domestic horror, of the beautiful heroism and devotedness too, of old Greek tragedy. His sister Mary, ten years his senior, in a sudden paroxysm of madness, caused the death of her mother, and was brought to trial for what an overstrained justice might have construed as the greatest of crimes. She was released on the brother's pledging himself to watch over her; and to this sister, from the age of twenty-one, Charles Lamb sacrificed himself, 'seeking thenceforth', says his earliest biographer, 'no connexion which could interfere with her supremacy in his affections, or impair his ability to sustain and comfort her'.[2] The 'feverish, romantic tie of love', he cast away in exchange for the 'charities of home'. Only, from time to time, the madness returned, affecting him too, once; and we see the brother and sister voluntarily yielding to restraint. In estimating the humour of *Elia*, we must no more forget the strong undercurrent of this great misfortune and pity, than one could forget it in his actual story. So he becomes the best critic, almost the discoverer, of Webster, a dramatist of genius so sombre, so heavily coloured, so *macabre*. *Rosamund Grey*, written in his twenty-third year, a story with something bitter and exaggerated, an almost insane fixedness of gloom perceptible in it, strikes clearly this note in his work.

For himself, and from his own point of view, the exercise of his gift, of his literary art, came to gild or sweeten a life of monotonous labour, and seemed, as far as regarded others, no very important thing; availing to give them a little pleasure, and inform them a little, chiefly in a retrospective manner, but in no way concerned with the turning of the tides of the great world. And yet this very modesty, this unambitious way of conceiving his work, has impressed upon it a certain exceptional enduringness. For of the remarkable English writers contemporary with Lamb, many were greatly preoccupied with ideas of practice—religious, moral, political—ideas which have since, in some sense or other, entered permanently into the general consciousness; and, these having no longer any stimulus for a generation provided with a different stock of ideas, the writings of those who spent so much of themselves in their propagation have lost, with posterity, something of what they gained by them in immediate influence. Coleridge, Wordsworth, Shelley even—sharing so largely in the unrest of their own age, and made personally more interesting thereby, yet, of their actual work, surrender more to the mere course of time than some of those who may have seemed to exercise themselves hardly at all in great matters, to have been little serious, or a little indifferent, regarding them.

Of this number of the disinterested servants of literature, smaller in England than in France, Charles Lamb is one. In the making of prose he realises the principle of art for its own sake, as completely as Keats in the making of verse. And, working ever close to the concrete, to the details, great or small, of actual things, books, persons, and with no part of them blurred to his vision by the intervention of mere abstract theories, he has reached an enduring moral effect also, in a sort of boundless sympathy. Unoccupied, as he might seem, with great matters, he is in immediate contact with what is real, especially in its caressing littleness, that littleness in which there is much of the whole woeful heart of things, and meets it more than half-way with a perfect understanding of it. What sudden, unexpected touches of pathos in him!—bearing witness how the sorrow of humanity, the *Weltschmerz*, the constant aching of its wounds, is ever present with him: but what a gift also for the enjoyment of life in its subtleties, of enjoyment actually refined by the need of some thoughtful economies and making the most of things! Little arts of happiness he is ready to teach to others. The quaint remarks of children which another would scarcely have heard, he preserves—little flies in the priceless amber of his Attic wit—and has his 'Praise of chimney-sweepers' (as William Blake has written, with so much natural pathos, the Chimney-sweeper's Song) valuing carefully their white teeth, and fine enjoyment of white sheets in stolen sleep at Arundel Castle, as he tells the story, anticipating something of the mood of our deep humourists of the last generation. His simple mother-pity for those who suffer by accident, or unkindness of nature, blindness for instance, or fateful disease of mind like his sister's, has something primitive in its largeness; and on behalf of ill-used animals he is early in composing a *Pity's Gift*.

And if, in deeper or more superficial sense, the dead *do* care at all for their name and fame, then how must the souls of Shakespeare and Webster have been stirred, after so long converse with things that stopped their ears, whether above or below the soil, at his exquisite appreciations of them; the souls of Titian and of Hogarth too; for, what has not been observed so generally as the excellence of his literary criticism, Charles Lamb is a fine critic of painting also. It was as loyal, self-forgetful work for others, for Shakespeare's self first, for instance, and then for Shakespeare's readers, that that too was done: he has the true scholar's way of forgetting himself in his subject. For though 'defrauded', as we saw, in his young years, 'of the sweet food of academic institution', he is yet essentially a scholar, and all his work mainly retrospective; as I said, his own sorrows, affections, perceptions, being alone real to him of the present. 'I cannot make these present times', he says once, 'present to *me*.'

Above all, he becomes not merely an expositor, permanently valuable, but for Englishmen almost the discoverer of the old English drama. 'The book is such as I am glad there should be', he modestly says of the *Specimens of English Dramatic Poets who lived about the time of Shakespeare*; to which, however, he adds in a series of notes the very quintessence of criticism, the choicest savour and perfume of Elizabethan poetry being sorted, and stored here, with a sort of delicate intellectual epicureanism, which has had the effect of winning for these, then almost forgotten, poets, one generation after another of enthusiastic students. Could he but have known how fresh a source of culture he was evoking there for other generations, through all those years in which, a little wistfully, he would harp on the limitation of his time by business, and sigh for a better fortune in regard to literary opportunities!

To feel strongly the charm of an old poet or moralist, the literary charm of Burton, for instance, or Quarles, or The Duchess of Newcastle; and then to interpret that charm, to convey it to others—he seeming to himself but to hand on to others, in mere humble ministration, that of which for them he is really the creator—this is the way of his criticism; cast off in a stray letter often, or passing note, or lightest essay or conversation. It is in such a letter, for instance, that we come upon a singularly penetrative estimate of the genius and writings of Defoe.

Tracking, with an attention always alert, the whole process of their production to its starting-point in the deep places of the mind, he seems to realise the but half-conscious intuitions of Hogarth or Shakespeare, and develops the great ruling unities which have swayed their actual work; or 'puts up', and takes, the one morsel of good stuff in an old, forgotten writer. Even in what he says casually there comes an aroma of old English; noticeable echoes, in chance turn and phrase, of the great masters of style, the old masters. Godwin, seeing in quotation a passage from *John Woodvil*, takes it for a choice fragment of an old dramatist, and goes to Lamb to assist him in finding the author. His power of delicate imitation in prose and verse reaches the length of a fine mimicry even, as in those late essays of Elia on Popular Fallacies, with their gentle reproduction or caricature of Sir Thomas Browne, showing, the more completely, his mastery, by disinterested study, of those elements of the man which were the real source of style in that great, solemn master of old English, who, ready to say what he has to say with fearless homeliness, yet continually overawes one with touches of a strange utterance from worlds afar. For it is with the delicacies of fine literature especially, its gradations of expression, its fine judgment, its pure sense of words, of vocabulary— things, alas! dying out in the English literature of the present, together with the appreciation of them in our literature of the past—that his literary mission is chiefly concerned. And yet, delicate, refining, daintily epicurean, as he may seem, when he writes of giants, such as Hogarth or Shakespeare, though often but in a stray note, you catch the sense of veneration with which those great names in past literature and art brooded over his intelligence, his undiminished impressibility by the great effects in them. Reading, commenting on Shakespeare, he is like a man who walks alone under a grand stormy sky, and among unwonted tricks of light, when powerful spirits might seem to be abroad upon the air; and the grim humour of Hogarth, as he analyses it, rises into a kind of spectral grotesque; while he too knows the secret of fine, significant touches like theirs.

There are traits, customs, characteristics of houses and dress, surviving morsels of old life, such as Hogarth has transferred so vividly into *The Rake's Progress*, or *Marriage à la Mode*, concerning which we well understand how, common, uninteresting, or even worthless in themselves, they have come to please us at last as things picturesque, being set in relief against the modes of our different age. Customs, stiff to us, stiff dresses, stiff furniture—types of cast-off fashions, left by accident, and which no one ever meant to preserve—we contemplate with more than good-nature, as having in them the veritable accent of a time, not altogether to be replaced by its more solemn and self-conscious deposits; like those tricks of individuality which we find quite tolerable in persons, because they convey to us the secret of life-like expression, and with regard to which we are all to some extent humourists. But it is part of the privilege of the genuine humourist to anticipate this pensive mood with regard to the ways and things of his own day; to look upon the tricks in manner of the life about him with that same refined, purged sort of vision, which will come naturally to those of a later generation, in observing whatever may have survived by chance of its mere external habit. Seeing things always by the light of an understanding more entire than is possible for ordinary minds, of the whole mechanism of humanity, and seeing also the manner, the outward mode or fashion, always in strict connexion with the spiritual condition which determined it, a humourist such as Charles Lamb anticipates the enchantment of distance; and the characteristics of places, ranks, habits of life, are transfigured for him, even now and in advance of time, by poetic light; justifying what some might condemn as mere sentimentality, in the effort to hand on unbroken the tradition of such fashion or accent. 'The praise of beggars', 'the cries of London', the traits of actors just grown 'old', the spots in 'town' where the country, its fresh green and fresh water, still lingered on, one after another, amidst the bustle; the quaint, dimmed, just played-out farces, he had relished so much, coming partly through them to understand the earlier English theatre as a thing once really alive; those fountains and sun-dials of old gardens, of which he entertains such dainty discourse:—he feels the poetry of these things, as the poetry of things old indeed, but surviving as an actual part of the life of the present, and as something quite different from the poetry of things flatly gone from us and antique, which come back to us, if at all, as entire strangers, like Scott's old Scotch-border personages, their oaths and armour. Such gift of appreciation depends, as I said, on the habitual apprehension of men's life as a whole—its organic wholeness, as extending even to the least things in it—of its outward manner in connexion with its inward temper; and it involves a fine perception of the congruities, the musical accordance between humanity and its environment of custom, society, personal intercourse; as if all this, with its meetings, partings, ceremonies, gesture, tones of speech, were some delicate instrument on which an expert performer is playing.

These are some of the characteristics of Elia, one essentially an essayist, and of the true family of Montaigne, 'never judging', as he says, 'system-wise of things, but fastening on particulars'; saying all things as it were on chance occasion only, and by way of pastime, yet succeeding thus, 'glimpse-wise', in catching and recording more frequently than others 'the gayest, happiest attitude of things'; a casual writer for dreamy readers, yet always giving the reader so much more than he seemed to propose. There is something of the follower of George Fox about him, and the Quaker's belief in the inward light coming to one passive, to the mere wayfarer, who will be sure at all events to lose no light which falls by the way—glimpses, suggestions, delightful half-apprehensions, profound thoughts of old philosophers, hints of the innermost reason in things, the full knowledge of which is held in reserve; all the varied stuff, that is, of which genuine essays are made.

And with him, as with Montaigne, the desire of self-portraiture is, below all more superficial tendencies, the real motive in writing at all —a desire closely connected with that intimacy, that modern subjectivity, which may be called the *Montaignesque* element in literature.[3] What he designs is to give you himself, to acquaint you with his likeness; but must do this, if at all, indirectly, being indeed always more or less reserved, for himself and his friends; friendship counting for so much in his life, that he is jealous of anything that might jar or disturb it, even to the length of a sort of insincerity, to which he assigns its quaint 'praise'; this lover of stage plays significantly welcoming a little touch of the artificiality of play to sweeten the intercourse of actual life.

And, in effect, a very delicate and expressive portrait of him does put itself together for the duly meditative reader. In indirect touches of his own work, scraps of faded old letters, what others remembered of his talk, the man's likeness emerges; what he laughed and wept at, his sudden elevations, and longings after absent friends, his fine casuistries of affection and devices to jog sometimes, as he says, the lazy happiness of perfect love, his solemn moments of higher discourse with the young, as they came across him on occasion, and went along a little way with him, the sudden, surprised apprehension of beauties in old literature, revealing anew the deep soul of poetry in things, and withal the pure spirit of fun, having its way again; laughter, that most short-lived of all things (some of Shakespeare's even being grown hollow) wearing well with him. Much of all this comes out through his letters, which may be regarded as a department of his essays. He is an old fashioned letter-writer, the essence of the old fashion of letter-writing lying, as with true essay-writing, in the dexterous availing oneself of accident and circumstance, in the prosecution of deeper lines of observation; although, just as with the record of his conversation, one loses something, in losing the actual tones of the stammerer, still graceful in his halting, as he halted also in composition, composing slowly and by fits, 'like a Flemish painter', as he tells us, so 'it is to be regretted', says the editor of his letters, 'that in the printed letters the reader will lose the curious varieties of writing with which the originals abound, and which are scrupulously adapted to the subject'.

Also, he was a true 'collector', delighting in the personal finding of a thing, in the colour an old book or print gets for him by the little accidents which attest previous ownership. Wither's *Emblems*, 'that old book and quaint', long-desired, when he finds it at last, he values none the less because a child had coloured the plates with his paints. A lover of household warmth everywhere, of that tempered atmosphere which our various habitations get by men's living within them, he 'sticks to his favourite books as he did to his friends', and loved the 'town', with a jealous eye for all its characteristics, 'old houses' coming to have souls for him. The yearning for mere warmth against him in another, makes him content, all through life, with pure brotherliness, 'the most kindly and natural species of love', as he says, in place of the *passion* of love. Brother and sister, sitting thus side by side, have, of course, their anticipations how one of them must sit at last in the faint sun alone, and set us speculating, as we read, as to precisely what amount of melancholy really accompanied for him the approach of old age, so steadily foreseen; make us note also, with pleasure, his successive wakings up to cheerful realities, out of a too curious musing over what is gone and what remains, of life. In his subtle capacity for enjoying the more refined points of earth, of human relationship, he could throw the gleam of poetry or humour on what seemed common or threadbare; has a care for the sighs, and the weary, humdrum preoccupations of very weak people, down to their little pathetic 'gentilities', even; while, in the purely human temper, he can write of death, almost like Shakespeare.

And that care, through all his enthusiasm of discovery, for what is accustomed, in literature, connected thus with his close clinging to home and the earth, was congruous also with that love for the accustomed in religion, which we may notice in him. He is one of the last votaries of that old-world sentiment, based on the feelings of hope and awe, which may be described as the religion of men of letters (as Sir Thomas Browne has his *Religion of the Physician*) religion as understood by the soberer men of letters in the last century, Addison, Gray, and Johnson; by Jane Austen and Thackeray, later. A high way of feeling developed largely by constant intercourse with the great things of literature, and extended in its turn to those matters greater still, this religion lives, in the main retrospectively, in a system of received sentiments and beliefs; received, like those great things of literature and art, in the first instance, on the authority of a long tradition, in the course of which they have linked themselves in a thousand complex ways to the conditions of human life, and no more questioned now than the feeling one keeps by one of the greatness—say! of Shakespeare. For Charles Lamb, such form of religion becomes the solemn background on which the nearer and more exciting objects of his immediate experience relieve themselves, borrowing from it an expression of calm; its necessary atmosphere being indeed a profound quiet, that quiet which has in it a kind of sacramental efficacy, work-ing, we might say, on the principle of the *opus operatum*, almost with-out any co-operation of one's own, towards, the assertion of the higher self. And, in truth, to men of Lamb's delicately attuned temperament mere physical stillness has its full value; such natures seeming to long for it sometimes, as for no merely negative thing, with a sort of mystical sensuality.

The writings of Charles Lamb are an excellent illustration of the value of reserve in literature. Below his quiet, his quaintness, his humour, and what may seem the slightness, the occasional or accidental character of his work, there lies, as I said at starting, as in his life, a genuinely tragic element. The gloom, reflected at its darkest in those hard shadows of *Rosamund Grey*, is always there, though not always realised either for himself or his readers, and restrained always in utterance. It gives to those lighter matters on the surface of life and literature among which he for the most part moved, a wonderful force of expression, as if at any moment these slight words and fancies might pierce very far into the deeper soul of things. In his writing, as in his life, that quiet is not the low-flying of one from the first drowsy by choice, and needing the prick of some strong passion or worldly ambition, to stimulate him into all the energy of which he is capable; but rather the reaction of nature, after an escape from fate, dark and insane as in old Greek tragedy, following upon which the sense of mere relief becomes a kind of passion, as with one who, having narrowly escaped earthquake or shipwreck, finds a thing for grateful tears in just sitting quiet at home, under the wall, till the end of days.

He felt the genius of places; and I sometimes think he resembles the places he knew and liked best, and where his lot fell—London, sixty-five years ago, with Covent Garden and the old theatres, and the Temple gardens still unspoiled, Thames gliding down, and beyond to north and south the fields at Enfield or Hampton, to which, 'with their living trees', the thoughts wander 'from the hard wood of the desk'—fields fresher, and coming nearer to town then, but in one of which the present writer remembers, on a brooding early summer's day, to have heard the cuckoo for the first time. Here, the surface of things is certainly humdrum, the streets dingy, the green places, where the child goes a-maying, tame enough. But nowhere are things more apt to respond to the brighter weather, nowhere is there so much difference between rain and sunshine, nowhere do the clouds roll together more grandly; those quaint suburban pastorals gathering a certain quality of grandeur from the background of the great city, with its weighty atmosphere, and portent of storm in the rapid light on dome and bleached stone steeples.

ROBERT ELSMERE[1]

Those who, in this bustling age, turn to fiction not merely for a little passing amusement, but for profit, for the higher sort of pleasure, will do well, we think (after a conscientious perusal on our own part) to bestow careful reading on *Robert Elsmere*. A *chef d'œuvre* of that kind of quiet evolution of character through circumstance, introduced into English literature by Miss Austen, and carried to perfection in France by George Sand (who is more to the point, because, like Mrs Ward, she was not afraid to challenge novel-readers to an interest in religious questions), it abounds in sympathy with people as we find them, in aspiration towards something better—towards a certain ideal—in a refreshing sense of second thoughts everywhere. The author clearly has developed a remarkable natural aptitude for literature by liberal reading and most patient care in composition—composition in that narrower sense which is concerned with the building of a good sentence; as also in that wider sense, which ensures, in a work like this, with so many joints, so many currents of interest, a final unity of impression on the part of the reader, and easy transition by him from one to the other. Well-used to works of fiction which tell all they have to tell in one thin volume, we have read Mrs Ward's three volumes with unflagging readiness. For, in truth, that quiet method of evolution, which she pursues undismayed to the end, requires a certain lengthiness; and the reader's reward will be in a secure sense that he has been in intercourse with no mere flighty remnants, but with typical forms, of character, firmly and fully conceived. We are persuaded that the author might have written a novel which should have been all shrewd impressions of society, or all humorous impressions of country life, or all quiet fun and genial caricature. Actually she has chosen to combine something of each of these with a very sincerely felt religious interest; and who will deny that to trace the influence of religion upon human character is one of the legitimate functions of the novel?[2] In truth, the modern 'novel of character' needs some such interest, to lift it sufficiently above the humdrum of life; as men's horizons are enlarged by religion, of whatever type it may be—and we may say at once that the religious type which is dear to Mrs Ward, though avowedly 'broad', is not really the broadest. Having conceived her work thus, she has brought a rare instinct for probability and nature to the difficult task of combining this religious motive and all the learned thought it involves, with a very genuine interest in many varieties of average mundane life.

We should say that the author's special ethical gift lay in a delicately intuitive sympathy, not, perhaps, with all phases of character, but certainly with the very varied class of persons represented in these volumes. It may be congruous with this, perhaps, that her success should be more assured in dealing with the characters of women than with those of men. The men who pass before us in her pages, though real and tangible and effective enough, seem, nevertheless, from time to time to reveal their joinings. They are composite of many different men we seem to have known, and fancy we could detach again from the *ensemble* and from each other.[3] And their goodness, when they are good, is—well! a little conventional; the kind of goodness that men themselves discount rather largely in their estimates of each other. Robert himself is certainly worth knowing—a really attractive union of manliness and saintliness, of shrewd sense and unworldly aims, and withal with that kindness and pity the absence of which so often abates the actual value of those other gifts. Mrs Ward's literary power is sometimes seen at its best (it is a proof of her high cultivation of this power that so it should be) in the analysis of minor characters, both male and female. Richard Leyburn, deceased before the story begins, but warm in the memory of the few who had known him, above all of his great-souled daughter Catherine, strikes us, with his religious mysticism, as being in this way one of the best things in the book:—

'Poor Richard Leyburn! Yet where had the defeat lain?

'"Was he happy in his school life?" Robert asked gently. "Was teaching what he liked?"

'"Oh! yes, only——" Catherine paused and then added hurriedly, as though drawn on in spite of herself by the grave sympathy of his look, "I never knew anybody so good who thought himself of so little account. He always believed that he had missed everything, wasted everything, and that anybody else would have made infinitely more out of his life. He was always blaming, scourging himself. And all the time he was the noblest, purest, most devoted——"

'She stopped. Her voice had passed beyond her control. Elsmere was startled by the feeling she showed. Evidently he had touched one of the few sore places in this pure heart. It was as though her memory of her father had in it elements of almost intolerable pathos, as though the child's brooding love and loyalty were in perpetual protest even now after this lapse of years against the verdict which an over-scrupulous, despondent soul had pronounced upon itself. Did she feel that he had gone uncomforted out of life—even by her—even by religion? Was that the sting?'

A little later she gives the record of his last hours:—

'"Catherine! Life is harder, the narrower way narrower than ever. I die"—and memory caught still the piteous long-drawn breath by which the voice was broken—"in much—much perplexity about many things. You have a clear soul, an iron will. Strengthen the others. Bring them safe to the day of account." '

And then the smaller—some of them, ethically, very small—women; Lady Wynnstay, Mrs Fleming, Mrs Thornburgh; above all, Robert's delightful Irish mother, and Mrs Darcy; how excellent they are! Mrs Darcy we seem to have known, yet cannot have enough of, rejoiced to catch sight of her capital letter on the page, as we read on. In truth, if a high and ideal purpose, really learned in the school of Wordsworth and among the Westmorland hills which Mrs Ward describes so sympathetically, with fitting dignity and truth of style, has accompanied the author throughout; no less plain, perhaps more pleasing to some readers, is the quiet humour which never fails her, and tests, while it relieves, the sincerity of her more serious thinking:—

'At last Mrs Darcy fluttered off, only, however, to come hurrying back with little, short, scudding steps, to implore them all to come to tea with her as soon as possible in the garden that was her special hobby, and in her last new summer-house.

'"I build two or three every summer", she said; "now there are twenty-one! Roger laughs at me", and there was a momentary bitterness in the little eerie face; "but how can one live without hobbies? That's one—then I've two more. My album—oh, you *will* all write in my album, won't you? When I was young —when I was Maid of Honour"—and she drew herself up slightly—"everybody had albums. Even the dear Queen herself! I remember how she made M. Guizot write in it; something quite stupid, after all. *Those* hobbies— the garden and the album—are *quite* harmless, aren't they? They hurt nobody, do they?" Her voice dropped a little, with a pathetic expostulating intonation in it, as of one accustomed to be rebuked.'

Mrs Ward's women, as we have said, are more organic, sympathetic, and really creative, than her men, and make their vitality evident by becoming, quite naturally, the centres of very life-like and dramatic *groups* of people, family or social; while her men are the very *genii* of isolation and division. It is depressing to see so really noble a character as Catherine soured, as we feel, and lowered, as time goes on, from the happy resignation of the first volume (in which solemn, beautiful, and entire, and so very real, she is like a poem of Wordsworth) down to the mere passivity of the third volume, and the closing scene of Robert Elsmere's days, very exquisitely as this episode of unbelieving yet saintly biography has been conceived and executed. Catherine certainly, for one, has no profit in the development of Robert's improved gospel. The 'stray sheep', we think, has by no means always the best of the argument, and her story is really a sadder, more testing one than his. Though both alike, we admit it cordially, have a genuine sense of the eternal moral charm of 'renunciation', something even of the thirst for martyrdom, for those wonderful, inaccessible, cold heights of the *Imitation*, eternal also in their æsthetic charm.

These characters and situations, pleasant or profoundly interesting, which it is good to have come across, are worked out, not in rapid sketches, nor by hazardous epigram, but more securely by patient analysis; and though we have said that Mrs Ward is most successful in female portraiture, her own mind and culture have an unmistakable virility and grasp and scientific firmness. This indispensable intellectual process, which will be relished by admirers of George Eliot, is relieved constantly by the sense of a charming landscape background, for the most part English. Mrs Ward has been a true disciple in the school of Wordsworth, and really undergone its influence. Her Westmorland scenery is more than a mere background; its spiritual and, as it were, *personal* hold on *persons*, as understood by the great poet of the Lakes, is seen actually at work, in the formation, in the refining, of character. It has been a stormy day :—

'Before him the great hollow of High Fell was just coming out from the white mists surging round it. A shaft of sunlight lay across its upper end, and he caught a marvellous apparition of a sunlit valley hung in air, a pale strip of blue above it, a white thread of stream wavering through it, and all around it and below it the rolling rain-clouds.'

There is surely something of 'natural magic' in that! The wilder capacity of the mountains is brought out especially in a weird story of a haunted girl, an episode well illustrating the writer's more imaginative psychological power; for, in spite of its quiet general tenour, the book has its adroitly managed elements of sensation—witness the ghost, in which the average human susceptibility to supernatural terrors takes revenge on the sceptical Mr Wendover, and the love-scene with Madame de Netteville, which, like those other exciting

passages, really furthers the development of the proper ethical interests
of the book. The Oxford episodes strike us as being not the author's
strongest work, as being comparatively conventional, coming, as they
do, in a book whose predominant note is reality. Yet her sympathetic
command over, her power of evoking, the genius of places, is clearly
shown in the touches by which she brings out the so well-known grey
and green of college and garden—touches which bring the real Oxford
to the mind's eye better than any elaborate description—for the
beauty of the place itself resides also in delicate touches. The book
passes indeed, successively, through distinct, broadly conceived phases
of scenery, which, becoming veritable parts of its texture, take hold on
the reader, as if in an actual sojourn in the places described. Surrey—
its genuine though almost suburban wildness, with the vicarage and
the wonderful abode, above all, the ancient library of Mr Wendover,
all is admirably done, the landscape naturally counting for a good
deal in the development of the profoundly meditative, country-loving
souls of Mrs Ward's favourite characters.

Well! Mrs Ward has chosen to use all these varied gifts and
accomplishments for a certain purpose. Briefly, Robert Elsmere, a
priest of the Anglican Church, marries a very religious woman; there
is the perfection of 'mutual love'; at length he has doubts about
'historic Christianity'; he gives up his orders; carries his learning,
his fine intellect, his goodness, nay, his saintliness, into a kind of
Unitarianism; the wife becomes more intolerant than ever; there is a
long and faithful effort on both sides, eventually successful, on the
part of these mentally divided people, to hold together; ending with
the hero's death, the genuine piety and resignation of which is the
crowning touch in the author's able, learned, and thoroughly sincere
apology for Robert Elsmere's position.

For good or evil, the sort of doubts which troubled Robert Elsmere
are no novelty in literature, and we think the main issue of the
'religious question' is not precisely where Mrs Ward supposes—that
it has advanced, in more senses than one, beyond the point raised by
Renan's *Vie de Jésus*.[4] Of course, a man such as Robert Elsmere came
to be ought not to be a clergyman of the Anglican Church. The priest
is still, and will, we think, remain, one of the necessary types of
humanity; and he is untrue to his type, unless, with whatever inevitable doubts in this doubting age, he feels, on the whole, the
preponderance in it of those influences which make for faith. It is his
triumph to achieve as much faith as possible in an age of negation.
Doubtless, it is part of the ideal of the Anglican Church that, under
certain safeguards, it should find room for latitudinarians even among
its clergy. Still, with these, as with all other genuine priests, it is the

positive not the negative result that justifies the position. We have little patience with those liberal clergy who dwell on nothing else than the difficulties of faith and the propriety of concession to the opposite force. Yes! Robert Elsmere was certainly right in ceasing to be a clergyman. But it strikes us as a blot on his philosophical pretensions that he should have been both so late in perceiving the difficulty, and then so sudden and trenchant in dealing with so great and complex a question. Had he possessed a perfectly philosophic or scientific temper he would have hesitated. This is not the place to discuss in detail the theological position very ably and seriously argued by Mrs Ward. All we can say is that, one by one, Elsmere's objections may be met by considerations of the same *genus*, and not less equal weight, relatively to a world so obscure, in its origin and issues, as that in which we live.

Robert Elsmere was a type of a large class of minds which cannot be sure that the sacred story is true. It is philosophical, doubtless, and a duty to the intellect to recognize our doubts, to locate them, perhaps to give them practical effect. It may be also a moral duty to do this. But then there is also a large class of minds which cannot be sure it is false—minds of very various degrees of conscientious and intellectual power, up to the highest. They will think those who are quite sure it is false unphilosophical through lack of doubt. For their part, they make allowance in their scheme of life for a great possibility, and with some of them that bare concession of possibility (the subject of it being what it is) becomes the most important fact in the world. The recognition of it straightway opens wide the door to hope and love; and such persons are, as we fancy they always will be, the nucleus of a Church. Their particular phase of doubt, of philosophic uncertainty, has been the secret of millions of good Christians, multitudes of worthy priests. They knit themselves to believers, in various degrees, of all ages. As against the purely negative action of the scientific spirit, the high-pitched Grey, the theistic Elsmere, the 'ritualistic priest', the quaint Methodist Fleming, both so admirably sketched, present perhaps no unconquerable differences. The question of the day is not between one and another of these, but in another sort of opposition, well defined by Mrs. Ward herself, between—

'Two estimates of life—the estimate which is the offspring of the scientific spirit, and which is for ever making the visible world fairer and more desirable in mortal eyes; and the estimate of Saint Augustine.'

To us, the belief in God, in goodness at all, in the story of Bethlehem, does not rest on evidence so diverse in character and force as Mrs Ward supposes. At his death Elsmere has started what to us would be a most unattractive place of worship, where he preaches an admirable sermon on the purely human aspect of the life of Christ. But we think there would be very few such sermons in the new church or chapel, for the interest of that life could hardly be very varied, when all such sayings as that 'though He was rich, for our sakes He became poor' have ceased to be applicable to it. It is the infinite nature of Christ which has led to such diversities of genius in preaching as St Francis, and Taylor, and Wesley.

And after all we fear we have been unjust to Mrs Ward's work. If so, we should read once more, and advise our readers to read, the profoundly thought and delicately felt chapter—chapter forty-three in her third volume—in which she describes the final spiritual reunion, on a basis of honestly diverse opinion, of the husband and wife. Her view, we think, could hardly have been presented more attractively. For ourselves we can only thank her for pleasure and profit in the reading of her book, which has refreshed actually the first and deepest springs of feeling, while it has charmed the literary sense.

A NOVEL BY MR OSCAR WILDE*[1]

There is always something of an excellent talker about the writing of Mr Oscar Wilde; and in his hands, as happens so rarely with those who practise it, the form of dialogue is justified by its being really alive. His genial, laughter-loving sense of life and its enjoyable intercourse, goes far to obviate any crudity there may be in the paradox, with which, as with the bright and shining truth which often underlies it, Mr Wilde, startling his 'countrymen', carries on, more perhaps than any other writer, the brilliant critical work of Matthew Arnold. *The Decay of Lying*, for instance, is all but unique in its half-humorous, yet wholly convinced, presentment of certain valuable truths of criticism. Conversational ease, the fluidity of life, felicitous expression, are qualities which have a natural alliance to the successful writing of fiction; and side by side with Mr Wilde's *Intentions* (so he entitles his critical efforts) comes a novel, certainly original, and affording the reader a fair opportunity of comparing his practice as a creative artist with many a precept he has enounced as critic concerning it.

A wholesome dislike of the common-place, rightly or wrongly identified by him with the *bourgeois*, with our middle-class—its habits and tastes—leads him to protest emphatically against so-called 'realism' in art; life, as he argues, with much plausibility, as a matter of fact, when it is really awake, following art—the fashion an effective artist sets; while art, on the other hand, influential and effective art, has never taken its cue from actual life. In *Dorian Gray* he is true certainly, on the whole, to the æsthetic philosophy of his *Intentions*; yet not infallibly, even on this point: there is a certain amount of the intrusion of real life and its sordid aspects—the low theatre, the pleasures and griefs, the faces of some very unrefined people, managed, of course, cleverly enough. The interlude of Jim Vane, his half-sullen but wholly faithful care for his sister's honour, is as good as perhaps anything of the kind, marked by a homely but real pathos, sufficiently

---

* 'The Picture of Dorian Gray'. By Oscar Wilde. (Ward, Lock and Co., London, New York, and Melbourne.)

pro⟨v⟩ g a versatility in the writer's talent, which should make his book popular. Clever always, this book, however, seems intended to set forth anything but a homely philosophy of life for the middle-class —a kind of dainty Epicurean theory, rather—yet fails, to some degree, in this; and one can see why. A true Epicureanism aims at a complete though harmonious development of man's entire organism.[2] To lose the moral sense therefore, for instance, the sense of sin and righteousness, as Mr Wilde's hero—his heroes are bent on doing as speedily, as completely as they can, is to lose, or lower, organisation, to become less complex, to pass from a higher to a lower degree of development. As a story, however, a partly supernatural story, it is first-rate in artistic management; those Epicurean niceties only adding to the decorative colour of its central figure, like so many exotic flowers, like the charming scenery and the perpetual, epigrammatic, surprising, yet so natural, conversations, like an atmosphere all about it. All that pleasant accessory detail, taken straight from the culture, the intellectual and social interests, the conventionalities, of the moment, have, in fact, after all, the effect of the better sort of realism, throwing into relief the adroitly-devised supernatural element after the manner of Poe, but with a grace he never reached, which supersedes that earlier didactic purpose, and makes the quite sufficing interest of an excellent story.

We like the hero, and, spite of his, somewhat unsociable, devotion to his art, Hallward, better than Lord Henry Wotton. He has too much of a not very really refined world in and about him, and his somewhat cynic opinions, which seem sometimes to be those of the writer, who may, however, have intended Lord Henry as a satiric sketch. Mr Wilde can hardly have intended him, with his cynic amity of mind and temper, any more than the miserable end of Dorian himself, to figure the motive and tendency of a true Cyrenaic or Epicurean doctrine of life. In contrast with Hallward, the artist, whose sensibilities idealise the world around him, the personality of Dorian Gray, above all, into something magnificent and strange, we might say that Lord Henry, and even more the, from the first, suicidal hero, loses too much in life to be a true Epicurean—loses so much in the way of impressions, of pleasant memories, and subsequent hopes, which Hallward, by a really Epicurean economy, manages to secure. It should be said, however, in fairness, that the writer is impersonal: seems not to have identified himself entirely with any one of his characters: and Wotton's cynicism, or whatever it be, at least makes a very clever story possible. He becomes the spoiler of the fair young man, whose bodily form remains un-aged; while his picture, the *chef d'œuvre* of the artist Hallward, changes miraculously with the

gradual corruption of his soul. How true, what a light on the artistic
nature, is the following on actual personalities and their revealing
influence in art. We quote it as an example of Mr Wilde's more
serious style.

'I sometimes think that there are only two eras of any importance in the
world's history. The first is the appearance of a new medium for art, and the
second is the appearance of new personality for art also. What the invention
of oil-painting was to the Venetians, the face of Antinous was to late Greek
sculpture, and the face of Dorian Gray will some day be to me. It is not
merely that I paint from him, draw from him, sketch from him. Of course I
have done all that. But he is much more to me than a model or a sitter. I
won't tell you that I am dissatisfied with what I have done of him, or that
his beauty is such that Art cannot express it. There is nothing that Art
cannot express, and I know that the work I have done, since I met Dorian
Gray, is good work, is the best work of my life. But in some curious way his
personality has suggested to me an entirely new manner in art, an entirely
new mode of style. I see things differently, I think of them differently. I can
now recreate life in a way that was hidden from me before.'

Dorian himself, though certainly a quite unsuccessful experiment
in Epicureanism, in life as a fine art, is (till his inward spoiling takes
visible effect suddenly, and in a moment, at the end of his story) a
beautiful creation. But his story is also a vivid, though carefully
considered, exposure of the corruption of a soul, with a very plain
moral, pushed home, to the effect that vice and crime make people
coarse and ugly. General readers, nevertheless, will probably care less
for this moral, less for the fine, varied, largely appreciative culture of
the writer, in evidence from page to page, than for the story itself,
with its adroitly managed supernatural incidents, its almost equally
wonderful applications of natural science; impossible, surely, in fact,
but plausible enough in fiction. Its interest turns on that very old
theme, old because based on some inherent experience or fancy of the
human brain, of a double life : of Döppelgänger—not of two *persons*, in
this case, but of the man and his portrait; the latter of which, as we
hinted above, changes, decays, is spoiled, while the former, through
a long course of corruption, remains, to the outward eye, unchanged,
still in all the beauty of a seemingly immaculate youth—'the devil's
bargain'. But it would be a pity to spoil the reader's enjoyment by
further detail. We need only emphasise, once more, the skill, the real
subtlety of art, the ease and fluidity withal of one telling a story by
word of mouth, with which the consciousness of the supernatural is
introduced into, and maintained amid, the elaborately conventional,
sophisticated, disabused world Mr Wilde depicts so cleverly, so
mercilessly. The special fascination of the piece is, of course, just

there—at that point of contrast. Mr Wilde's work may fairly claim to go with that of Edgar Poe, and with some good French work of the same kind, done, probably, in more or less conscious imitation of it.

Notes

Coleridge's Writings

1 *Westminster Review*, January 1867, reprinted in *Appreciations*, 1889. The latter version excludes some biographical detail and adds the study of Coleridge's poetry which Pater had contributed to T. H. Ward's *English Poets*, 1888. The changes in the 1889 version reflect Pater's modification of his early anti-Christian approach, although he maintains his belief in relativism as the surest mode of ascertaining truth. Significant passages omitted in 1889 are marked with square brackets.

2 Incorporated into the concluding section of the 1889 version. Writing there on Coleridge's poetry Pater sees it as marked still more strongly than his prose by his 'morbid languor of nature'. He concentrates on Coleridge's duality, the contrasts in his personality and work, 'tropical touches in a chilly climate'. Relating the concepts of Fancy and the Imagination to the poetry Pater finds that in rare instances Coleridge approaches the impassioned contemplation of Wordsworth. He particularly admires the minute realism of passages in such poems as 'Dejection', 'Christabel' and 'The Ancient Mariner', and the last two are seen also to appeal to 'that taste for the supernatural, that longing for the *frisson*, a shudder, to which the romantic school in Germany and its derivatives in England and France, directly ministered'. Cp. 'Postscript'. But it is the 'delicacy, the dreamy grace' which makes Coleridge's work on the supernatural so remarkable.

3 The idea of the modern age as introspective and burdened with reflection is a common theme. Cp. 'Winckelmann' (pp. 35–6), 'Postscript' (p. 53), 'Du Bellay' (p. 92), 'Lamb' (p. 130).

4 For a description of Asiatic qualities see 'The Marbles of Ægina'.

5 An extreme view which Pater had wholly rejected by the time he came to write *Marius the Epicurean* (1885).

6 See Raysor, *Coleridge's Shakespearian Criticism*, 1936. (Vol. I, p. 198.)

7 Pater's most definite statement of the ability of humanistic culture to replace traditional religion.

Winckelmann

1 The complete study (published in the *Westminster Review*, January 1867, reprinted 1889 in *Appreciations*), opens with a brief study of Winckelmann's life (1717–68) and art criticism.

2 Pater now examines the growth of art from Greek religion and society. He argues that all religions contain a basic 'pagan sentiment' compounded of sadness and fear in the face of death and the unknown. To combat such insecurity fixed rituals are created and from ritual grows the creation of myth and the embodiment of the religious ideal in sensuous form. The Hellenic desire to 'incarnate', in contrast to the medieval tendency to symbolize spiritual ideas, combined with the Greek love of beauty, leads to expression in sculpture rather than in any other art. In its limitation to pure form, sculpture can reveal 'not what is accidental in man, but the god, as opposed to man's restless movement'.

3 Arnold. 'Maurice de Guérin', *Essays in Criticism*, 1865.

4 In his *Æsthetik*, referred to earlier in the essay, Hegel propounds a series of artistic developments: the first stage is 'symbolic', as in architecture; the second 'classical', best expressed in sculpture; the last 'romantic', finding expression in painting, music and poetry.

Conclusion to 'The Renaissance'

1 *The Renaissance*, 1873. The 'Conclusion' and 'Æsthetic Poetry' were originally published as parts of 'Poems by William Morris', *Westminster Review*, November 1868. It was withdrawn from the second edition and reinstated in the third (1888) in a more tentative form, with all direct allusions to religion altered (see notes). Pater added a note explaining that he had dealt more fully with the thoughts raised by it in *Marius the Epicurean*, 1885. (Vol. I, Chs. VIII and IX). In the novel his sensationalism is placed in an established philosophical tradition, descending from Greek Cyrenaicism and its Roman counterpart Epicureanism. The charge of hedonism which had been levelled against the 'Conclusion' is countered by the claim that culture is an education in perception 'till one's whole nature becomes one complex medium of reception, towards the vision—the "beatific vision"—if one really cared to make it such— of our actual experiences in the world'.

2 'Somewhere Heraclitus says that all things vanish and nothing remains fixed.' Plato, *Phaedrus*.

3 1888. 'driven in many currents'.

4 1888. 'The service of philosophy, of speculative culture, toward the human spirit . . .'

5 1888. 'In a sense it may be said that our failure . . .'
6 1888. 'Philosophical theories or ideas, as points of view . . .'
7 1888. 'The various forms of enthusiastic activity, disinterested or otherwise, which come naturally to many of us.'
8 Some interesting comments on the influence of Pater's philosophy of culture upon the writers and poets of the 'Nineties may be found in Yeats's *Autobiographies*, 1926.

The School of Giorgione

1 First published in the *Fortnightly Review*, October 1877, reprinted in *The Renaissance* (3rd edition), 1888.
2 1776. Lessing divided the arts into those of time (music and literature) and space (painting and sculpture).
3 For an example of Pater's analysis of correspondences between art forms see 'Joachim du Bellay' (pp. 83–4).
4 Pater uses music as a symbol of cosmic and artistic harmony. It is in this sense that great art provides a sense of unity in a seemingly chaotic world, cp. *Plato and Platonism*. 'To realise unity in variety, to discover *cosmos*—an order that shall satisfy one's reasonable soul—below and within apparent chaos; is from first to last the continuous purpose of what we call philosophy. Well Pythagoras seems to have found that unity of principle (ἀρχή) in the dominion of number everywhere, the harmony, the music, into which number as such expands.'

Postscript to 'Appreciations'

1 First published as 'Romanticism' in *Macmillan's Magazine*, November 1876.
2 'He praises the ancient wine, while lauding the pick of the newer things.'
3 This fleeting and deprecatory reference to Racine illustrates the extent to which Pater was influenced by the critical prejudices of his age and of his Romantic precursors despite his claim to seek æsthetic value in the works of all ages, without preconceptions.
4 Pater deals with Provençal poetry at greater length in 'Two Early French Stories', *The Renaissance*, 1873. In that study he develops the paradox that it was the 'romantic' strain, curiosity and a spirit of rebellion, which led to the rediscovery of classical literature and culture preceding the Renaissance. This, and the description of Rousseau's romanticism in the 'classical' eighteenth century, are good examples of his theory that each epoch, while it has a specific cultural identity, also contains opposing or balancing elements.
5 Pater's only considered criticism of Dante appears in his introduction to *The Purgatory of Dante Alighieri*. Ed. Shadwell, 1892.

The Marbles of Ægina

1 First published in the *Fortnightly Review*, February 1880. Reprinted in *Greek Studies*, 1895.
2 E.g. Overbeck in *Die Antiken Schriftquellen*, 1865.
3 Pater's argument focuses on the contrast between the 'Ionian' religion centred around vegetation myths and the 'Doric' religion of Apollo; 'a sanction of, and an encouragement towards the true valuation of humanity in its sanity, its proportion, its knowledge of itself'. The contrast had already been discussed in K. O. Muller's *History and Antiquities of the Doric Race*. Trans. Tufnell & Lewis, 1830.

Style

1 First published in *Appreciations*, 1889.
2 An extension to literature of the discussion on *Anders-streben* between art forms. Cp. 'The School of Giorgione' (p. 45).
3 Despite Pater's insistence in this essay on the removal of 'surplus-age' (p. 68) he greatly enjoyed the extravagant styles of seventeenth-century prose writers. In fact he finds much of their charm lies in their very lack of personal and stylistic restraint: 'Hence their amazing pleasantry, their indulgence in their own conceits; but hence also those unpremeditated wild flowers of speech we should never have the good luck to find in any more formal type of literature.' 'Sir Thomas Browne', *Appreciations*, 1889.
4 *Essays on the Poets*. (Pope)
5 The essay on Pascal (*Miscellaneous Studies*, 1895) repeats many of the dicta of 'Style'. Pater sees Pascal's greatness as a writer in the exact relation of his style to the quality of his argument: 'The brevity, the discerning edge, the impassioned concentration of the language are here one with the ardent, immediate apprehensions of his spirit'.
6 Cp. *Plato and Platonism*, where Pater defines the essay as the literary correlative of the relative spirit and identifies this form with the genius of Montaigne: 'It provided him with precisely the literary form necessary to a mind for which truth itself is but a possibility, realisable not as a general conclusion, but rather as the elusive effect of a particular personal experience.'
7 Saintsbury later provided an interesting analysis of Pater's own prose in *History of English Prose Rhythm*, 1912.
8 His own scholarly attentiveness is illustrated by the innumerable textual changes in various editions of his work. The third edition of *Marius* contains three thousand alterations (see Chandler, *Pater on Style*, 1958). For further illustration of Pater's interest in language cp. 'Joachim du Bellay' (pp. 86–7), and see *Marius the Epicurean*, Ch. VI, 'Euphuism'.

9 Pater's admiration of Flaubert is also expressed in two uncollected reviews, 'The Life and Letters of Flaubert', *Pall Mall Gazette*, August 1888 and 'Correspondence of Gustave Flaubert 1850–4', *Athenaeum*, August 1889.

Preface to 'The Renaissance' (1873)

1 Cp. Matthew Arnold, 'On Translating Homer', 1861, restated in *The Function of Criticism at the Present Time*, 1865: 'Of the literature of France and Germany, as of the intellect of Europe in general, the main effort, for now many years, has been a critical effort: the endeavour, in all branches of knowledge, theology, philosophy, history, art, science, to see the object as in itself it really is.'

2 Cp. Ruskin, *Modern Painters*, 1843. 'That which is required in order to the attainment of accurate conclusions respecting the Essence of the beautiful is nothing more than earnest, loving and unselfish attention to our impressions of it, by which those that are shallow, false or peculiar to times and temperaments, may be distinguished from those that are eternal.' Third edition, 1851. (Vol. II, Part i, Ch. 3.)

3 A marginal annotation to the works of Sir Joshua Reynolds. The precise quotation is: 'Ages are all equal but genius is always above the age.'

4 See 'Wordsworth'.

The Genius of Plato

1 First published in *Contemporary Review*, February 1892. Reprinted in *Plato and Platonism*, 1893.

Joachim du Bellay

1 *The Renaissance*, 1873.

2 For a discussion of correlation between the arts see 'The School of Giorgione' (pp. 43–7).

3 An imaginative appreciation of Ronsard's life and influence can be found in *Gaston de Latour*, Ch. III, 'Modernity'.

4 Hegel. See 'Winckelmann', Note 4 and Introduction.

5 Voluntary exile and homesickness are a constant motif in Pater's fiction. The theme recurs in his criticism, acting as an image of the sense of insecurity when a writer or critic is cut off from his appropriate material or setting, and also as an image of general insecurity in the face of death once religious certainties have disappeared. Cp. 'Coleridge' (p. 26), 'Æsthetic Poetry' (p. 95).

6 The interest of the French Romantics in medieval poetry parallels that of English nineteenth-century poets discussed in 'Æsthetic Poetry'.

7 Lang, *Ballads and Lyrics of Old France*, 1872. The 'grace' Pater finds
in Lang's translations is largely due to unnecessary alliteration
which in no way reproduces the quality of the original.

Æsthetic Poetry

1 *Appreciations*, 1889. Omitted from second and later editions. First
published as part of 'Poems by William Morris', *Westminster
Review*, 1868.

2 This point is also made in 'Two Early French Stories', *The
Renaissance*, 1873.

3 This is the theme of the imaginary portrait 'Apollo in Picardy',
1893, *Miscellaneous Studies*, 1895.

Wordsworth

1 First published in the *Fortnightly Review*, April 1874. Reprinted in
Appreciations, 1889.

2 1879, *Poems of Wordsworth*, Chosen and edited by Matthew Arnold,
1888, *Selections from Wordsworth*. By W. Knight and other members of
the Wordsworthian Society.

3 The 'penetrative' power of the imagination in nineteenth-century
painting is stressed in Ruskin's *Modern Painters*, 1843: 'It is its
reaching, by intuition and intensity of gaze . . . a more essential
truth than is seen at the surface of things.' Third edition, 1851.
(Vol. II, Part ii, Ch. 3.)

4 An oversimplification ignoring Wordsworth's intense emotional
involvement with the French Revolution, his affair with Annette
Vallon, etc.

5 A strange comparison, ignoring the very different quality of the
imagery in the two poems.

6 Pater treats the subject of animism and of religious conservatism in
Greek Studies, 1895.

'Measure for Measure'

1 First published in the *Fortnightly Review*, November 1874. Reprinted
in *Appreciations*, 1889.

2 See Raysor op. cit., Vol. I, p. 102. Coleridge found that 'the comic
and the tragic parts equally border on the μιςητόν, the one
disgusting, the other horrible'.

3 Tennyson. *Mariana, Mariana in the South.*

4 This sense of man's helplessness in the web of circumstance
and influence beyond his control recalls 'Winckelmann' (p. 37),
while the plea for a finer justice based on 'a more delicate
appreciation of the true condition of men and things', echoes

Pater's initial assertion in 'Coleridge' (p. 2) that the relative spirit must break down moral absolutes.

Charles Lamb

1 First published in the *Fortnightly Review*, October 1878.
2 T. N. Talfourd. *Letters of Charles Lamb*, 1837. 2 vols. with biography.
3 A portrait of Montaigne appears in Gaston de Latour, Chs. IV and V. It provides an illuminating commentary on Pater's critical attitudes as outlined in the 'Preface' and on his championship of the essay as the appropriate modern form. Montaigne's egotism is seen as the inevitable result of, and only escape from, the solipsism of the 'Conclusion', the predicament of modern man: 'It was the recognition, over against, or in continuation of, that world of floating doubt, of the individual mind, as for each one severally, at once the unique organ, and the only matter, of knowledge—the wonderful energy, the reality and authority of that, in its absolute loneliness, conforming all things to its law, without witnesses as without judge, without appeal, save to itself.'

'Robert Elsmere'

1 First published in *The Guardian*, 28th March 1888. Reprinted in *Essays from the Guardian*, 1901.
2 The publication of *Robert Elsmere* led to a controversy in current periodicals because of the assertion in the novel that Christianity could survive as an ethical code shorn of its miraculous elements. Pater's rejection of this idea shows how far he had moved from the materialism of 'Coleridge'.
3 This may be literally true. Mrs Ward was Matthew Arnold's niece and a friend of Pater and it was suggested that several characters in the novel were based on contemporary Oxford figures and that of Edward Langham, a 'languid sensationalist', on Pater himself. Pater had reviewed Mrs Ward's translation of Amiel's *Journal Intime* in *The Guardian*, March 1886.
4 Ernest Renan (1823–92). The point raised in the *Vie de Jésus*, 1863, is exactly that put forward in the novel (note 1). Mrs Ward had reviewed Renan's autobiography in 1883 and specifically identifies Elsmere's loss of faith with Renan's own doubts.

A Novel by Mr Oscar Wilde

1 *The Bookman*, November 1891.
2 An interesting justification, towards the end of Pater's literary career, of his early philosophy in *The Renaissance*.

Index of Names